"From the moment you open Ruth's book, *Cooking with Love: Recipes from an Israeli Home,* you know you have entered into a special world, one that thrives on her love of food, cooking, and family. Not only is Ruth a skilled cook with numerous recipes from an Israeli kitchen, she brings forth in this book informative chapters on cutting down on fat, tips on staying healthy, and notes on making stocks, salads, fish and meats. Ruth manages to impart such a warm personal style that you feel as if you grew up in her home town in Israel and traveled with her to Europe and America during her university days where her culinary world expanded. It is this blending of her personal experience with a deep knowledge and love of food and cooking that makes her work truly a joyous labor of love."

Richard LaMarita
Chef Instructor/Writer
National Gourmet Institute for Health and Culinary Arts

Ruth Mishkin

COOKING
WITH LOVE

Ventures into the New Israeli Cuisine

COOKING
WITH LOVE

RUTH MILSTEIN

Tate Publishing & *Enterprises*

Cooking With Love
Copyright © 2008 by Ruth Milstein. All rights reserved.

This title is also available as a Tate Out Loud product. Visit www.tatepublishing.com for more information.

No part of this publication may be reproduced, stored in a retrieval system or transmitted in any way by any means, electronic, mechanical, photocopy, recording or otherwise without the prior permission of the author except as provided by USA copyright law.

The opinions expressed by the author are not necessarily those of Tate Publishing, LLC.

Published by Tate Publishing & Enterprises, LLC
127 E. Trade Center Terrace | Mustang, Oklahoma 73064 USA
1.888.361.9473 | www.tatepublishing.com

Tate Publishing is committed to excellence in the publishing industry. The company reflects the philosophy established by the founders, based on Psalm 68:11,
"The Lord gave the word and great was the company of those who published it."

Book design copyright © 2008 by Tate Publishing, LLC. All rights reserved.
Cover design by Lindsay B. Behrens
Interior design by Kellie Southerland
Photography by Sasha Gitin of Sasha Gitin Photography
*Red Rice photo on page 215 by Ruth Milstein

Published in the United States of America

ISBN: 978-1-60604-263-2
1. Cooking   2. Regional & Ethnic: International
08.07.16

To my loving family, who introduced me to the
treasures that good food brings to our daily lives.

To the light of my life and my inspiration:
my husband.

INTRODUCTION

There were fruit trees in our backyard: apricot, plum, pear, avocado, mandarin, and lemon. We had a vegetable garden and flowers of every color the rainbow grew there. From the terrace, we could sit and enjoy this display of nature's beauty and abundance every day. The kitchen was the first room as you entered the house from the terrace, and my mother, after teaching class in high school, was often there preparing some dish for our lunch or dinner or for a holiday coming up, using the fruits and vegetables from our backyard. The aroma of food cooking permeated the house when she was in the kitchen.

My earliest memories are of these delicious aromas: eggplants roasting on the stovetops, meat stewing all day in a large pot, or fruits cooking down with sugar to be made into jam.

For holidays she would start to assemble her ingredients and make salads or condiments planning the meal days in advance. The anticipation of her meal by our family and friends would be overwhelming; no one missed the opportunity to sit at our dining table for one of her meals.

The kitchen was a gathering place for our family when she worked there. I loved to sit at the large kitchen table, always covered in a colorful cloth, and watch her or talk to her and my sisters about my day as she cooked. There was always a bowl of fresh fruit, nuts, or some pastries on the table to nibble on and sometimes she instructed us as to what she was doing. "Quality creates quality," she said, referring to her most basic principle in the kitchen of using only the freshest, finest ingredients. When she asked me to help her in the kitchen, I felt privileged and excited. At first we gathered fruit off the trees or picked vegetables from the garden together or I would wash some produce or do simple cutting or stirring of a pot, but soon my mother was encouraging me to prepare a whole dish. "'You cook the rice tonight, Ruth," or "Can you make the potato dish?" she would say. And before I knew it, I was preparing simple dishes under her watchful eye. She was my first teacher in the kitchen and instilled in me a love of cooking that is very much alive today.

We lived in B'Nai Braq, an ancient city mentioned in the Bible, about ten miles east of Tel Aviv. B'Nai Braq is a very orthodox city, although we considered ourselves much more traditional. My father did want us home early, however, on the eve of the Sabbath, mostly out of respect for our neighbors, and we did keep a kosher home. I still observe Sabbath eve and my cooking remains kosher to this day, although I long ago dropped many other influences of my childhood there when I went to university in the more cosmopolitan Tel Aviv and traveled frequently in Europe and America. Yet, due to my early habits in the kitchen and out of respect for Jewish religious law, we do not mix dairy and meat. This law stems from the belief that one should avoid the possibility of eating an animal mixed with the milk of another animal that might have been its mother. The book presented here is strictly kosher. However, kosher here does not mean traditional Jewish holiday cooking, nor does it imply that the food of Israel cannot be delicious and varied. There is a distinct and delicious cuisine that we can call Israeli.

Growing up in, Israel, I soon realized the diversity of my country. Although small in size, (Israel is about the size of New Jersey or Belgium), the inhabitants of present-day Israel come from eighty different countries. People who later settled in what is known from biblical days as the land of milk and honey are from eastern Europe and Russia, the Middle and Near East, Northern, Africa, and even from Asia. Surprisingly, for such a small nation, our geography is varied ranging from the now-blooming desert in the south, the hills and valleys in the north, and the Mediterranean along the west coast.

Israeli cuisine and culture reflects this diversity. The lush and fertile north provides the freshest fruits and vegetables imaginable; you have never tasted a peach or orange so juicy and sweet until you taste one from Israel. Many of my vegetable dishes reflect this reliance on freshness and simplicity, such as the zucchini with walnuts or the radish and apple salad that perfectly unites the sweet and tart of the apple with the pungency of the radish. There is also a bold use of fruit in dishes with poultry, fish, or meat that brings surprising results. The south is a tourist area like Florida in the United States. Today, you can find all sorts of food in this region, which was once a parched desert. Along the coast, fish is abundant and combined creatively with fruit and vegetables. Try the salmon in an orange sauce; the combination is wonderful.

Additionally, the diverse cultural groups of Israel have created a diversified cuisine dictated by customs and religious law. Jews remain faithful to a kosher table. 'The Yemen' Jews from the desert and the Middle Eastern Jews rely on grilled meats and hearty stuffed vegetables. Eastern European Jews have brought schnitzel, goulash and blintzes to Israel. Jews from Arab countries have created a fine Middle Eastern cuisine consisting of falafel, grain salad, hummus, and flatbreads that is known worldwide. All these diversified influences have blended together into a cuisine that we can call Israeli. I have borrowed, liberally, from all these influences.

Israelis love salads. Not just the green salads with vinaigrettes that we are familiar with here in the United States, but salads of all sorts made with meats or poultry, vegetables, grains, and fruits. Two great Israeli customs provide a perfect expression for this love: the Israeli breakfast and the outdoor family picnic where salads outnumber the family members two to one to accompany the grilled meats. The day starts early on a picnic day when everyone gathers at the home of a family member for coffee and then together drive an hour or so to a picnic spot in a shady park or along the sea. The tables are arranged in a long line, the charcoals are lit, and soon the men begin their all-day grilling, and every family member unwraps and presents their prepared salads: eggplant, potato, carrot, chicken, mushroom, artichoke, avocado, mango, apple, wherever the imagination and skill take you. The day is long and the drive home at night is slow, but there is a feeling of love and satisfaction that is unequaled. I looked forward to this tradition on my visits home during my university years.

I attended Tel Aviv University where I studied art and journalism. As part of my studies, I traveled often to Europe, particularly England

and the Netherlands, as well as the United States. In these countries, I explored other ethnic cuisine. I was especially drawn to Asian and Indian foods because of the exotic blend of spices and ingredients used. Ginger, chili, peppers, saffron, soy sauce, cumin, and coriander all became part of my repertoire. On one stay in London, I picked up a wok and brought it back home with me. No one in my family had seen one before and asked what it was and how to use it.

During this time in Israel, Chinese restaurants began to appear in all the major cities and I frequented them often. One day I discovered an Indonesian recipe for a dish using Asian spices in a unique and interesting way. On my own that afternoon, I completed the dish and presented it to my family at mealtime; they were surprised at my effort and the new and different tastes they encountered. For me, however, it was a memorable accomplishment because it was the first really complex recipe that I had found and completed. I felt that for the first time, an expression of myself and of who I am came out in the food.

Having always thought of myself as an innovative person, I have always enjoyed exploring and interpolating things to suit my tastes and personality. In cooking, when I see a recipe, I absorb it, think about it, and then might add a little here or add a little there.

My mother encouraged me to experiment and, in effect, taught me to believe in myself in the kitchen and in life. As a result, my dishes, whether prepared for my family or for my friends when I was in college or living abroad, were instantly recognizable. "Ruth made this dish," I would overhear someone say as they tasted food from a banquet table for a holiday. I would be the one who added pineapple to the rice or olives and raisins in the chicken dish.

This sense of wonder and experimentation in the kitchen gave me encouragement as a young girl and throughout my life, has continued to be my strength and style. I love the exotic and the traditional. In this cookbook, you will find classic dishes from the diverse traditions of the Israeli people. Other times, I add a modern or exotic twist to the recipe. I have also added standards and classic American comfort food such as meat loaf and mashed potatoes that my husband and friends have enjoyed over the years and would be disappointed if I left out of this work. I hope you enjoy these recipes, and please feel free to change them to add your own personal touch.

These are the recipes that I have accumulated over the years, written on scraps of paper or index cards. Some of these dishes I have improvised on from foods that I had surprisingly discovered through dining out, newspaper clippings and my extensive travels from around the world.

This is the food I love. I hope you enjoy it too!

CONTENTS

What is Kosher?		17
Cutting Down on Cholesterol and Fat		19
Some Notes on Fruits and Vegetables		23
Healthy Handling of Foods		25
Useful Substitutions		27
Temperature		29
Liquid Measure Equivalents		30
Dry Measures		31
Utensils		33
Appetizers		41
Soups		55
Salad and Vegetable Dishes		79
MAIN DISHES		103
Poultry		105
Beef		121
Lamb		135
Veal		141
Fish		147
Pies		169
Pasta		193
Rice		205
Breads and Rolls		217
Tofu		231
Sauces		245
Dips, Spreads, And Dressing		261
Beverages, Sherbets, and Compotes		275
Jams		287
Desserts		293
Entertaining		321
Substitutes		343

WHAT IS KOSHER?

The laws of kosher eating are complex. A few basics for keeping a kosher kitchen are given below.

- The fundamental law of keeping kosher is that meat and milk or milk products cannot be cooked or consumed together.

- When meat is consumed, one must wait a period of up to six hours before eating dairy. However, people should follow their family and community tradition, as some allow eating dairy following meat in one to three hours.

- When eating dairy first one must wait before eating meat only if the dairy consumed was a hard cheese.

- Separate utensils should be used for meat and dairy products.

- Both meat and dairy are allowed to be stored in the same refrigerator; however, care should be taken to avoid dripping from one to the other.

- Fish that have fins and scales are kosher. If the scales can be removed without damaging the skin, the fish is considered kosher. In this context, swordfish and shark are not kosher because by removing their scales, the skin is damaged. All shellfish is not kosher.

- When buying fish one should buy from a vendor that understands the laws of keeping kosher. Otherwise, contamination could occur by use of utensils, such as knives and cutting boards that were used in the preparation of fish that is not kosher.

- Fish may be cooked in either a meat or dairy pot and eaten with the corresponding cutlery.

CUTTING DOWN
ON CHOLESTEROL & FAT

The classic Mediterranean diet is considered one of the healthiest in the world because of its reliance on fresh foods, the use of fruits and vegetables, and being low in fat. Normally, when we think of this diet, we think of the foods of Italy, Southern France, and Spain. However, the Israeli diet certainly fits into this category and, by virtue of this and the fact that it also lies on the Mediterranean, we can consider the Israeli cuisine Mediterranean.

In this book, I have used numerous techniques to keep the recipes low in fat content. Here are some tips on how you can cut down on cholesterol and fat.

Use egg substitutes that now come frozen or powdered. These products are cholesterol-free and can be purchased in your local supermarkets. Use them for omelets or mixed with vegetables or meat, etc.

- When cooking omelets, you can use egg whites only.
- When baking, substitute two egg whites for one whole egg.
- Choose to eat skinless poultry. This can cut fat content by three-quarters and calories by half.

Use lean red meat and trim off fat. To remove half of the fat from ground beef, place the beef in a microwave-proof bowl and microwave it for 2 minutes, then strain the fat.

Use a substitute mayonnaise made from tofu. It is delicious. The recipe can be found in this cookbook.

To remove fat from soup, stew, sauce, or gravy, refrigerate overnight. The fat will rise to the top and congeal, making it easier to remove.

To reduce the amount of oil while you fry or sauté, get the pan hot before adding the oil. Then add a small amount and it will spread more easily and heat up quickly. The hotter the oil, the shorter the cooking time. Less fat will be absorbed by the food. Don't let the oil burn, however, by letting it smoke. Also, use healthy oils like extra-virgin olive oil.

When reading recipes, watch for terms that are giveaways to fatty food: creamed, crispy, breaded, a la king, carbonara, croquettes, parmigiana, tempura, fritters, alfredo, au gratin, batter-dipped, béchamel, hollandaise, and béarnaise.

Add poppy seeds to your green salads, in addition to olive oil. Poppy seeds are low in fat and calories and give a rich, nutty texture.

To lower cholesterol, eat beans, lentils, and dried peas. They are good sources of fiber, too.

Cut down on salt. Choose condiments wisely. Ketchup and mustard are high in sodium.

Use a salt substitute. See recipe in this cookbook.

Instant soups and stocks are usually loaded with sodium. If you choose to eat them, try the new instant soup versions, which are lower in fat and salt.

Add a few drops of fresh lemon juice to foods. This will perk up flavor and a give a little salt more bounce.

SOME NOTES ON
FRUITS & VEGETABLES

To get the most nutrients from fruits and vegetables:

Choose dark greens. They are loaded with vitamin B, C, Beta Carotene, and Folacin.

Potato skin has more fiber, iron, potassium and B vitamins than the flesh. Baking a potato in a microwave is easy and fast, only 6-8 minutes. Wash the skin carefully and eat the potato with the skin.

The most nutritious fruits and vegetables are broccoli, kale, carrots, red bell pepper, spinach, sweet potato, pumpkin, cantaloupe, mango, and strawberries. Other nutritious vegetables include cabbage, cauliflower, collard greens, and brussel sprouts. Many fruits and vegetables have anti-oxidants, which have been found to be effective in preventing cancer.

If certain fruits or vegetables are not in season, try frozen fruits and vegetables. They are delicious and nutritious for a snack or for baking.

To increase the amount of iron from food, consume drinks rich in vitamin C with your meal such as orange, grapefruit, or tomato juice.

Eat sweet potatoes. They have the same amount of calories as white potatoes, but double the amount of Beta Carotene and vitamin C.

To boost your calcium, eat sardines and canned salmon with their small bones.

Drink carrot juice. This juice has much Beta Carotene and vitamin C. Also eat fresh carrots, so you do not lose the fiber.

Sprinkle parsley on top of salad and cooked food. It is not only a garnish, but contains relatively high amounts of Beta Carotene, vitamin C, iron, and other minerals.

Always steam your vegetables instead of boiling them. Vegetables lose most of their mineral content through boiling.

Choose bright and dark-colored fruits and vegetables. The dark color is generally a sign of extra nutrients.

HEALTHY
HANDLING OF FOODS

Most food borne illnesses come from improper handling of foods. This can easily be prevented with some care and knowledge. Here are some tips on how to keep bacteria out of your food.

Wash all equipment, including cutting boards and countertops, which come in contact with food, especially raw meats and fish.

Do not let cooked food or refrigerator foods sit at room temperature.

Thaw frozen foods in the refrigerator on a low shelf overnight, in cold running water, or in a microwave.

Keep infused oils, particularly those with food matter in them, in the refrigerator. Whether commercial or homemade, if left at room temperature these oils could produce toxins that cannot be detected by taste or smell.

Guidelines for cooking eggs are 1.) Boil an egg in its shell at 140° for 3 ½ minutes to kill all bacteria. 2.) Scrambled eggs and omelets are fine if cooked past the runny, moist stage. 3.) Frying eggs "over easy" for 3 minutes on one side then 1 minute on the other is best preparation for eggs.

Marinate meat in the refrigerator only. Do not put cooked meat or poultry back into uncooked meat marinade. Do not serve the used marinade as a table sauce since it can become contaminated from the raw meat.

Handle ground meats carefully. Once ground, the meat has more surface area than a whole cut, making it an easier target for bacteria to form.

Tofu buyers beware: choose only commercially sealed packages, not the type floating in open trays of water.

Pack raw meat and poultry separately from fruit and vegetables at the market. This avoids any meat juices from leaking on the produce, which can cause contamination.

Wash all fruits and vegetables with antibacterial soap and rinse with a water mixture of a half cup vinegar with 2 quarts water.

Wipe up all juices from uncooked chicken or meat. These juices may contain bacteria, which leads to salmonella. Use a paper towel, not a sponge or dishcloth, to clean up the juices. A sponge can spread bacteria on dishes or surfaces, even the next day. If you choose to use a sponge, throw it immediately in the dishwasher for washing and for 2 minutes in the microwave for drying. This will kill all the bacteria.

USEFUL SUBSTITUTIONS

If the recipe calls for:	Use instead:
2 cups chicken or beef broth	1 small bouillon cube or 1 envelope or 1 teaspoon bouillon powder + 2 cups boiling water
6 cups chicken or beef broth	1 large bouillon cube or 3 envelopes or 3 teaspoons + 6 cups boiling water
1 teaspoon lemon juice	½ teaspoon distilled vinegar
1 teaspoon fresh herb	½ teaspoon dry herb
1 ounce unsweetened chocolate	3 tablespoons cocoa + 1-tablespoon butter or margarine

½ cup butter or margarine	7 tablespoons vegetable shortening
1 cup sour cream (for use in cooking)	⅓ cup butter + ¾ cup yogurt or buttermilk or 1 tablespoon lemon juice + evaporated milk to make 1 cup
1 teaspoon grated lemon peel	½ teaspoon lemon extract
1 egg	2 egg whites or 2 egg yolks
1 teaspoon baking powder	½ teaspoon cream of tartar + ½ teaspoon baking soda
2 tablespoons flour (thickening)	1 tablespoon cornstarch or potato starch

TEMPERATURE

CELSIUS	**FAHRENHEIT**	
-18° C	0° F	freezer temperature
0° C	32° F	freezing point of water
4° C	40° F	refrigerator temperature
29° C	85° F	yeast dough rises
38° C	100° F	lukewarm to touch
43° C	110° F	scalding hot
82° C	180° F	simmering point of water
95° C	200° F	warming oven
100° C	212° F	boling point of water
120° C	250° F	very slow oven
150° C	300° F	slow oven
165° C	325° F	moderately slow oven
180° C	350° F	moderate oven
190° C	375° F	moderately hot oven
205° C	400° F	hot oven
230° C	450° F	very hot oven
260° C	500° F	oven broiling

LIQUID MEASURE
EQUIVALENTS

1 gallon:	4 quarts	8 pints	16 cups	128 fluid ounces	3.79 liters
½ gallon:	2 quarts	4 pints	8 cups	64 fluid ounces	1.89 liters
¼ gallon:	1 quart	2 pints	4 cups	32 fluid ounces	0.95 liter
⅛ gallon:	½ quart	1 pint	2 cups	16 fluid ounces	0.47 liter
1/16 gallon:	¼ quart	½ pint	1 cup	8 fluid ounces	0.24 liter
1/32 gallon:	⅛ quart	¼ pint	½ cup	4 fluid ounces	0.12 liter

DRY MEASURES

1 cup:	8 fluid ounces	16 Tablespoons	48 teaspoons	237 milliliters
¾ cup:	6 fluid ounces	12 Tablespoons	36 teaspoons	177 milliliters
⅔ cup:	5 ⅓ fluid ounces	10 ⅔ Tablespoons	32 teaspoons	158 milliliters
½ cup:	4 fluid ounces	8 Tablespoons	24 teaspoons	118 milliliters
⅓ cup:	2 ⅔ fluid ounces	5 ⅓ Tablespoons	16 teaspoons	79 milliliters
¼ cup:	2 fluid ounces	4 Tablespoons	12 teaspoons	59 milliliters
⅛ cup:	1 fluid ounce	2 Tablespoons	6 teaspoons	30 milliliters
		1 Tablespoon	3 teaspoons	15 milliliters

Metric	**Imperial**
5 millimeters	¼ inch
2 centimeters	¾ inch
2.5 centimeters	1 inch
5 centimeters	2 inches
10 centimeters	4 inches

Metric	**Imperial**
28.4 grams	1 ounce
115 grams	¼ pound
230 grams	½ pound
454 grams	1 pound (16 ounces)
1 kilograms (1,000 grams)	2.2 pounds
2.2 kilograms	5 pounds

UTENSILS

Cooking Utensil	Metric	Imperial
	(Diameter x depth)	
Round cake pan	20 x 4 centimeters	8 x 1.5 inches
Round cake pan	23 x 4 centimeters	9 x 1.5 inches
Square Pyrex pan	20 x 5 centimeters	8 x 2 inches
Small Pyrex pan	18 x 28 x 5 centimeters	7x 11 x 2 inches
Large Pyrex pan	20 x 36 x 5 centimeters	8 x 14 x 2 inches
Small pie plate	20 centimeters	8 x 1.25 inches
Medium pie plate	23 centimeters	9 x 1.5 inches
Large pie plate	25 centimeters	10 x 1.75 inches
Loaf bread pan	11 x 21 x 7 centimeters	4.5 x 8.5 x 3 inches
Casserole	1 liter (15 centimeters)	1 quart (6 inches)
Casserole	2 liters (21 centimeters)	2 quart (8.5 inches)
Casserole	2.5 liters (23 centimeter)	2.5 quart (9 inches)
Casserole	3 liters (25 centimeter)	3 quart (10 inches)
Spring form pan	23 centimeters	9.25 x 2.5 inches
Spring form pan	25 centimeters	10 x 2.5 inches

for more information or to place an order, contact:

Tate Publishing & *Enterprises*

www.tatepublishing.com/bookstore
888.361.9473

Now Available

Ventures into the New Israeli Cuisine

COOKING WITH LOVE

RUTH MILSTEIN

RUTH MILSTEIN

COOKING WITH LOVE

r3mor@aol.com

Ruth Milstein

Colorful Pepper Basket
p. 326

Red Rice
p. 214

Watermelon Ice
p. 279

Burger
p. 126

Chicken Salad with Mango
& Pineapple p. 42

Ginger Dip With Apples & Pears
p. 266

Red Snapper Baked in Vegetables
p. 148

Seasoned Hot Wine
p. 276

Frosted Orange Cake
p. 306

Avocado Tofu Dessert
p. 241

Beef Stew with Red Wine
p. 130

Baked Pasta
p. 202

Cream of Carrot Soup
p. 74

Pumpkin Bread
p. 226

Fudge Chocolate Layer Cake
p. 295

Chicken in Orange & Kumquats
p. 114

APPETIZERS

Chicken Salad with Mango & Pineapple

Makes 6 servings

There are many plantations on the Kibbutzim in Israel that grow the most wonderful fruits and vegetables. Most are in the northern part of the country. Mangoes come out in early spring and pineapples are available all year round. The sweetness, texture, and juice of these fruits are simply oozing in flavor! Israelis love to mix fruits with poultry, meat, and fish. I created this dish as a holiday appetizer to highlight the fresh fruit in a light, refreshing style.

1 cup cooked chicken, sliced into 1-inch length and ⅛-inch width
1 green apple, cut into ½-inch cubes
1 8-ounce can pineapple, drained and cut into ¼- inch cubes
1 medium-sized mango, cut into ½-inch cubes
2 tablespoons mayonnaise
1 tablespoon lemon juice
1 tablespoon pineapple juice, from can
1 tablespoon orange liqueur

Combine chicken and fruits. Mix mayonnaise, lemon juice, pineapple juice, and liqueur.
Pour sauce over chicken mixture.
Cover and refrigerate for 2 hours to blend flavors.

APPETIZERS

Persimmon, Avocado, & Banana Salad

Makes 8 servings

When I was a child, we had a persimmon and avocado tree in our backyard. I remember seeing the fruit, but not knowing how to eat it. My mother showed me one day and soon after created this tasty salad. You wouldn't think of combining these fruits, but the final outcome is wonderful.

4 persimmons, sliced
4 medium-sized avocado, sliced
4 medium-sized banana, sliced

Sauce:
¼ cup honey
½ cup sunflower oil
1 green onion
5 tablespoons white wine vinegar
½ teaspoon Dijon mustard
1 tablespoon poppy seed

In large bowl mix gently the persimmon, the avocado and the banana.
Cover and chill for 2 hours.
In blender, puree all the sauce ingredients except poppy seed.
Add the poppy seed into the sauce.
Transfer to a bowl and cover. Refrigerate to blend flavor for 2 hours.
Divide the fruits into cocktail glasses and pour the sauce on top.

Chicken Livers in Apple Sauce

Makes 4 servings

Here I enhance the sweetness of the liver with the flavor of the apple.

- 2 tablespoons oil
- 1 large onion, thinly sliced
- 1 garlic clove, crushed
- 1 pound chicken livers, fresh or frozen and defrosted
- 4 ounces apple sauce
- 1 teaspoon honey
- ¼ cup dry red wine
- Salt and black pepper
- 1 pound fresh mushrooms, sliced

Simmer the oil in a large frying pan and sauté the onion until golden brown.
Add the garlic and the chicken livers and sauté a few minutes.
Take out the livers only and lay them aside.
Add to the frying pan the apple sauce, honey, and the wine. Season with salt and pepper.
Put the chicken livers back in the frying pan and add the mushrooms.
Cook for 15 minutes on low heat.
Serve hot on a bed of toast.

Potatoes & Portobello Mushroom

Makes 8 servings

Sometimes, I like to use Portobello mushrooms in place of meat. This simple dish is a perfect substitute for meat and potatoes. This exquisite recipe must be tasted to be believed.

2 ounces butter
2 tablespoons olive oil
2 minced garlic cloves
1 tablespoon fresh rosemary leaves
2 pounds potatoes, cut into 1-inch cubes
3 Portobello mushrooms, cut into 1-inch cubes
Salt, freshly ground black pepper
3 tablespoons minced parsley for garnish

Put the butter and the oil in a large and deep ovenproof frying pan. When the oil is hot, put in the garlic, the rosemary, and potatoes and sauté until the potatoes turn somewhat brown. Add the mushrooms, salt, and pepper.
Mix and continue to sauté for 2 minutes.
Cover the pan with aluminum foil and bake at 350° for 25 minutes until the potatoes turn soft. Transfer to a serving platter and garnish with minced parsley.
Serve hot with green salad.

Creamy Potato Salad

Makes 6 servings

2 pounds potatoes
2 tablespoons cider or white wine vinegar
½ teaspoon salt
½ cup finely chopped celery
½ cucumber, peeled and diced
½ cup finely chopped green onion
1 teaspoon dried sage or dried mint leaves
½ cup mayonnaise
4 tablespoons chopped parsley

Cook unpeeled potatoes in boiling salted water and cover for 20–30 minutes until tender.
Drain, peel while warm.
Cut potatoes into ½- inch cubes.
Sprinkle potatoes with cider vinegar and salt.
Gently mix in celery, cucumber, onions, sage, and 2 tablespoons parsley.
Gently fold mayonnaise into mixture.
Transfer to serving bowl and garnish with the remaining 2 tablespoons of parsley.
Cover and refrigerate to blend flavors for 2 hours.

String Beans with Smoked Turkey Breast

Makes 4 servings

1 pound fresh string beans
3 tablespoons olive oil
1 clove garlic, minced
1 teaspoon fresh ginger root, minced
2 ounces smoked turkey breast, cut up into thin, wide strips
1 teaspoon freshly ground black pepper
2 tablespoons soy sauce

Clean and cut the beans ends.
In a deep frying pan put 2 tablespoons oil and sauté the string beans for 3–4 minutes.
Take out and strain.
Put in a frying pan the remaining 1 tablespoon of oil. Sauté the garlic, ginger, and smoked turkey breasts. Sauté until the meat is brownish and crisp.
Add the strings beans and stir.
Add pepper and soy sauce. Stir and cook for about 2 minutes.
Transfer to a serving platter and serve immediately.

Ginger Flavored Asparagus

Makes 4 servings

I was introduced to ginger upon arriving in America when I frequented Asian restaurants. Its strong, yet elegant flavor compliments the asparagus.

1 pound asparagus, tough end snapped, cut into 2-inch pieces
2 teaspoons fresh ginger, minced
2 teaspoons sesame oil
2 tablespoons fresh lemon juice
Dash of salt and black pepper

Steam the asparagus until crisply tender for about 3-5 minutes.
Transfer to a serving bowl with the rest of the ingredients, season with salt and pepper.
Stir well.
Salad can be served cold, warm, or room temperature.
To serve cold, cover and chill for 1 hour.
To serve warm, serve immediately.
To serve room temperate, let cool for 30 minutes.
Serve with whole wheat bread.

Avocado & Potato Salad

Makes 6 servings

The love of avocado brought about this interesting salad of similar textures. The spiciness in the ginger and chili pepper perfectly contrasts with the softness in the potatoes and avocado.

    1 ½ pounds red skinned potatoes
    3 green onions, sliced
    1 teaspoon chives, minced
    1 hot chili pepper, seeded and minced
    1 teaspoon fresh ginger, minced
    1 tablespoon parsley, chopped
    Juice from 1 lemon
    1 large ripe, firm avocado, cut into ½ inch cubes

Slice the potatoes about ½-inch thick and place in a large pot.
Cover with water and bring to a boil. Lower the heat and simmer until tender, about 7 minutes.
Drain and let cool.
In a large mixing bowl, place potatoes, onions, chives, chili pepper, the parsley, and the lemon juice and stir gently.
Cover and refrigerate to blend flavor for 3 hours.
Add the avocado to the potato mixture just before serving.

Fried Mushrooms with Mayonnaise Sauce

Makes 6 servings

18 mushrooms
½ cup flour
1 egg, beaten
¼ cup bread crumbs
2 tablespoons oil
Sauce:
3 tablespoons mayonnaise
2 tablespoons sour cream
1 tablespoon capers
1 teaspoon fresh lemon
¼ teaspoon salt
¼ teaspoon black pepper

Dip the mushrooms first in flour, then in egg and finally in the bread crumbs.
Fry the mushroom in oil on medium heat 5-7 minutes.
Transfer to a serving platter.
Sauce:
In small bowl, mix all the ingredients and pour to a serving sauce bowl.
Serve hot.

Pastrami Salad with Potatoes

Makes 6 servings

My husband loves cold cuts. This is a great summer dish, easy and quick to prepare, where the fresh cold meat combines well with various vegetables for a meal in itself.

½ pound pastrami, cut into ¼-inch cubes
1 pound cooked potato, cut into ½-inch cubes
2 hard-boiled eggs, sliced
1 cucumber, cut into ¼-inch cubes
1 tomato, cut into ½-inch cubes
1 pickle, sliced
2 tablespoons mayonnaise
Dash of salt and pepper
2 tablespoons snipped parsley

Mix all ingredients. Cover and refrigerate to blend flavors for 3 hours. Before serving, sprinkle with parsley.

Beef Liver in Apples & Potatoes

Makes 4 servings

In this dish the combination of liver, potatoes, and onions is combined with the tartness of a sour apple. Again, an unconventional mixture of ingredients brings an amazingly delicious recipe.

- 2 tablespoons olive oil
- 2 large onions, minced
- 1 pound beef liver
- Salt and black pepper
- 1 cup beef or chicken broth
- ½ pound potatoes, peeled and minced
- 2 granny smith apples, peeled and sliced

Heat 1 tablespoon of the oil in a wide pot and sauté the minced onion until golden brown.
Take the onion out of pot.
Slice the liver to ½-inch thickness and sprinkle salt and pepper.
Add the rest of the oil to the pot, and sauté the liver slices on both sides.
Add the broth, the potatoes, the apples, and the onions.
Bring to a boil. Cover the pot, lower the heat, and simmer for 30 minutes.
Serve immediately.

Asparagus in Saffron Sauce

Makes 4 servings

Saffron is a delicate, wonderful spice that is often cooked in rice in Israel to add color and subtle flavor. It is quite expensive because of the labor-intensive work it takes to harvest. Saffron is the tiny, orange stigma of the crocus plant. Thankfully, only a few threads are necessary when used in a dish. I came up with this delicate saffron sauce to be placed on early spring asparagus. This sauce will add a touch of royalty to the asparagus.

1 cup dry white wine
2 tablespoons white wine vinegar
2 shallots, or 3 green onions, white only, minced
1 thyme stem, leaves only
10 whole peppercorns
½ teaspoon saffron (threads)
4 ounces heavy cream
3 ounces soft butter, cut into cubes
½ teaspoon fresh lemon juice
Salt, freshly ground black pepper
20 fresh asparagus stems
3 tablespoons minced chives

In a small pot, pour the wine, vinegar, onions, thyme, peppercorns, and the saffron.
Bring to a boil. Cook on low heat 3 minutes until there is hardly any liquid remaining in the pot.
Immediately add the heavy cream; mix, bring to a boil, and cook a few minutes, until the cream thickens somewhat.
Slowly add the butter, while mixing, until it all melts. (Add the lemon juice to slow down the cooking process.)
Season with salt and pepper.
Steam the asparagus for 2 minutes and arrange them on a serving platter.
Pour the sauce and sprinkle the chives on top.
Serve hot.

SOUPS

Using stocks as a base liquid for your soups will add an extra dimension of flavor, depth, and richness that cannot be attained when you use water. Here are some tips about stocks as well as simple recipes for beef, chicken, and vegetable stock.

When you can, always favor stocks over water, except if the soup is a bean soup. Then the water in which the beans were cooking will become rich and flavorful.

Store-bought stocks are getting better. Pacific brand stocks, sold in health food stores, are excellent. They currently make a vegetable, chicken, and mushroom.

In specialty markets, freshly-made stocks of all varieties are available.

Powdered stocks and bouillon cubes are acceptable, but be careful, as they tend be salty.

Stocks can be made in advance and in large quantities and then frozen. I like to freeze them in quart or pint containers or doubled zip-locked bags for easy defrosting.

Chicken Stock

1 tablespoon olive oil
3-4 pounds chicken parts (including neck and back)
    or 1 whole chicken
2 medium onions, large sliced
2-3 carrots cut in large chunks
2-3 celery ribs with leaves, in large chunks
1 head garlic
1 bay leaf
3 black peppercorns
2 sprigs thyme
2 sprigs parsley
1 whole allspice

In a large stockpot, place all ingredients, except edible parts of chicken. Add olive oil and cook for a few minutes. Add cold water and bring to a boil. Cook slightly covered and simmer for 15 minutes.

Add remainder of chicken and continue to simmer for 30–45 minutes until juices run clear or the dark meat can be pierced with fork. Strain, cool, and skim fat.

Beef Stock

1 tablespoon olive oil
4-6 pounds beef bones or shank
2 medium onions, in large slices
3 carrots cut in large chunks
3 celery ribs with leaves, cut in large chunks
2-3 tomatoes, chopped
1 head garlic
3 bay leaves
1 teaspoon dried thyme
12 black peppercorns
1 whole allspice
1 cup white or red wine

Preheat oven to 400°. In a heavy roasting pan, heat oil over high heat. Add the beef bones, onion, carrots, celery, tomatoes, and garlic. Place in oven and roast for 45 minutes-1 hour.

Take out of oven and place in large stockpot. Add bay leaves, thyme, peppercorns, allspice, wine and about 6 quarts of water (enough to cover the ingredients by 2"). Bring to boil, skimming off foam. Partially cover and cook for 3-5 hours over low heat. Strain, cool, and skim off fat. (For best results, refrigerate one day, then spoon off the top layer of fat.)

Vegetable Stock

1 tablespoon olive oil
2 medium onions
3 medium shallots, sliced
3 carrots cut in medium chunks
3 celery ribs with leaves, cut in medium chunks
1 small head of garlic
Any other vegetables that is available
6 parsley sprigs
2 bay leaves
10 peppercorns
2 sprigs thyme
2 cloves

Place ingredients in large stockpot with olive oil and sauté for a few minutes.
Add about 6 quarts water (enough to cover by 2"). Bring to boil, skimming off foam. Partially cover and cook for 1 hour over low heat. Strain, cool, and skim off any fat.

Spinach & Garlic Soup

Makes 6 servings

The fresh spinach and the pungent garlic together create an alluring flavor, a rich, savory texture and a deep, enticing color. A wonderful soup.

4 cups water
1 lemon zest
15 garlic cloves, peeled
½ pound potatoes, peeled and sliced
1 tablespoon fresh basil leaves, minced
½ teaspoon dried thyme leaves
1 tablespoon olive oil
½ teaspoon nutmeg
1 pound fresh spinach, cut into strips
Salt and pepper
Juice of ½ a lemon
1 8-ounce container plain yogurt

In a large pot, put in the water, the lemon zest, the garlic, the potatoes, the basil leaves, the thyme, the oil, and the nutmeg. Bring to a boil. Lower the heat and simmer for about 20 minutes.
Add the spinach to the pot and bring to a boil again. Cook for 5 minutes.
Strain the soup and put only the liquid back into the pot. In a food processor, puree the cooked vegetables, or mash through a strainer.
Put the mixture back to the pot with the liquid and bring the soup to a boil.
Season with salt, pepper, and lemon juice.
Transfer to a serving bowl and put 2 tablespoons yogurt into each bowl. Serve very hot with fresh French bread.

Mushroom Soup

Makes 6 servings

A hearty, rustic soup that is deep and woodsy in flavor and texture. Caramelize the onions first in oil for a more intensely rich flavor.

    1 pound fresh mushrooms
    1 ounce dry mushrooms, soaked in water for ½ hour
    1 Portobello mushroom, about 10 ounces
    4 medium-sized onions
    ½ cup olive oil or 4 ounces butter
    2 ½ cups water
    1 cube chicken-flavored bouillon
    ½ teaspoon salt
    ½ teaspoon white pepper
    Heavy cream to taste
    1 tablespoon minced dill for garnish

Slice all the mushrooms and mince the onions.
Put the oil or the butter in a large pot; sauté the onion until it turns translucent.
Add the mushrooms and continue to cook a few more minutes.
Add the water and the chicken-flavored bouillon; cook until the mushrooms become soft, or about 20 minutes.
Season with salt and pepper.
Pour into serving bowls. Add heavy cream, as per taste. And sprinkle with minced dill.
Serve hot with fresh whole wheat bread.

Carrot Soup

Makes 6 servings

6 carrots, thinly sliced
2 potatoes cut into small cubes
1 small onion, minced
2 ounces margarine
½ teaspoon salt
¼ teaspoon white pepper
¼ teaspoon sugar
1 cube chicken-flavored bouillon
5 cups water
Minced parsley for garnish

Peel the carrots, place them into a food processor, and shred them with the shredding disk.
In a large pot, put the potatoes, the onion, and 1 ounce margarine. Season with salt, pepper, and sugar.
Cook over a small heat for 15 minutes.
Dissolve the chicken-flavored bouillon cube in 2 tablespoons hot water and add to the pot. Add the water.
Cook without a cover for 20 minutes.
Take the vegetables out of the pot. Place them into a blender or food processor and puree until smooth. Put the pureed vegetables back in the pot.
Warm up the soup again. Add the remaining margarine and bring to a boil. Transfer to a serving bowl and garnish with parsley.
Serve with toasted bread.

Meatball Vegetable Soup

Makes 4 servings

*Meat and poultry soups can be used as appetizers or main dishes depending on your needs. Lighter based soups are preferable to begin the meal, while the full-bodied soups, like this soup, are more suitable with meat, so they can be enjoyed as full meal.

    1 pound lean ground beef
    1 egg
    1 small onion, thinly chopped
    1 teaspoon salt
    ½ teaspoon black pepper
    8 green onions
    4 cups beef broth, or 4 cups water and 1 cube beef-flavored bouillon, dissolved in 3 tablespoons hot water
    ¾ cup thinly sliced carrots
    ¾ cup thinly sliced celery
    ½ head cabbage, shredded
    2 tomatoes cut into eighths
    1 48-ounce can of tomato juice
    2 bay leaves
    2 teaspoons dried basil leaves
    2 tablespoons light soy sauce
    2 tablespoons chopped parsley for garnish

Blend the ground beef with the egg, chopped onion, salt, and pepper.
Cut green onions into ½-inch lengths and set aside.
Bring broth to a boil. Shape meat into 1-inch balls and drop them into broth.
Add the green onions, carrots, celery, cabbage, tomatoes, tomato juice, bay leaves, and basil. Cover and simmer for 30 minutes. Stir occasionally.
Discard bay leaves and stir in the soy sauce.
Before serving, sprinkle with parsley.

Lima Bean Soup

Makes 4 servings

Improvising on a kosher fava bean soup I had tasted in New York helped me to create a soup that is simply delicious.

   1 cup dried baby lima beans
   8 cups water
   ½ cup chopped onion
   3 cloves garlic, minced
   1 tablespoon margarine
   1 carrot, chopped
   ¼ cup chopped parsley
   ½ teaspoon each dried basil leaves and dried thyme
   ½ teaspoon black pepper
   ½ teaspoon salt

In large saucepan, simmer water and beans for 1 hour.
In skillet sauté onion and 1 minced clove garlic in margarine. Stir in carrot, herbs, and pepper. Set aside.
After beans have cooked for 1 hour, stir in vegetable mixture.
Cover and simmer for 30 minutes.
Put half of the beans in blender with some of the liquid, the parsley, and the remaining minced garlic clove and blend until smooth and pureed.
Combine puree with remaining soup. Add salt. Simmer for 15 minutes.
Serve hot with toasted whole wheat bread and a green salad.

Split Pea Soup

Makes 8 servings

2 tablespoons oil
1 medium-sized onion, minced
1 medium-sized carrot, sliced ½-inch thick
6 dill stems, minced
1 pound dry split peas
12 cups boiling water
½ teaspoon salt
¼ teaspoon black pepper
1 teaspoon cumin
1 tablespoon chicken-flavored bouillon

Heat the oil in a large wide pot.
Add the minced onion and sauté for 2–3 minutes.
Add the carrot, the dill, and the split peas and stir well.
Pour in water and add the chicken bouillon. Stir and cook on medium heat for about an hour.
Season with salt, pepper and cumin.
Continue to cook for about 30 minutes.
If you want a thicker soup, you may mash half of the split peas with a masher inside the soup. You may also process the entire soup in a food processor into a silky texture and then return the mixture to the pot and simmer for 2 minutes.
Serve hot with toasted bread.

Cauliflower Soup

Makes 6 servings

My husband's favorite vegetable, this creamy, chunky soup is served frequently in our house. Its hearty, rich character is almost a meal in itself. The luscious textures combined with the spices make this a truly winning dish.
*May be served hot or chilled

1 head cauliflower, broken into florets
1 large onion, chopped
1 teaspoon caraway seeds
6 cups water
½ teaspoon salt
¼ teaspoon white pepper
1 cup heavy cream
Chopped chives for garnish

In large saucepan, place cauliflower, onion, caraway seeds, and water. Cover and simmer for 20 minutes until cauliflower is tender but not mushy.
Place cooked cauliflower into food processor or blender. Add 1 cup soup and process until smooth and pureed.
Transfer the mixture into saucepan, add salt and pepper. Simmer for 15 minutes.
If eaten hot, add cream just before serving. Mix well for 1 minute on low heat and garnish with chopped chives.
If served chilled, refrigerate for 3 hours, and add the cream right before serving. Blend well and garnish with chives.
Serve with chicken and hot noodles.

Pumpkin Soup with Orange Scent

Makes 4 servings

We grew pumpkins in our backyard in Israel and my mother would use them to make a simple pumpkin soup or a stew made from chicken, pumpkin, and dried fruits. When I came to the United States, I saw how abundant they were in the fall and began cooking them in various dishes. In this soup, I added the orange zest to accent its gorgeous autumn flavor. This soup is a gourmet's health delight.

- 4 tablespoons olive oil
- 1 large onion, minced
- 1½ pounds pumpkin, cut up into small cubes
- 1 peeled potato, cut up into cubes
- ½ grated orange peel
- 4 cups chicken broth or water
- Salt and white pepper
- 2 tablespoons margarine
- 2 ounces pumpkin seeds, peeled and roasted

Warm up the oil in a pot and sauté the onion until translucent.
Add the pumpkin and the potato and sauté for 5 minutes.
Add the orange peel, the chicken broth or water, salt, and pepper and bring to a boil. Cook on a low heat for 15 minutes.
Transfer the soup to the blender, add the margarine, and make a smooth puree.
Distribute to the serving bowls and garnish with pumpkin seeds.
Serve hot or cold.
You can make thicker soup by mixing 1 tablespoon of corn flour with 2 tablespoons of water. Proceed to add this into the soup before you transfer to the blender.

Leek & Potato Soup

Makes 6 servings

Improvising on a soup I had in a New York restaurant, I created this soup that has now become one of our favorites at home. The ingredients used in this soup give a delectable, personal touch.

2 tablespoons margarine
1 leek, the white and green part cut up into thick slices
1 carrot, cut up into thick slices
¼ small cauliflower, separated to isolated flowers
2 peeled potatoes cut up into thick slices
4 cups clear chicken broth, possibly from 1 cube
    chicken-flavored bouillon dissolved in 2 tablespoons hot water
½ teaspoon salt
¼ teaspoon white pepper
2 tablespoons minced chives

Heat up the margarine in a large pot and sauté the leek on a low heat until it softens up.
Add the carrots and cauliflower and sauté while stirring for 2–3 minutes.
Add the potatoes and mix; pour the chicken broth into the pot, season with salt and pepper. Cover and bring to a boil. Lower the heat and simmer for 25–30 minutes or until the vegetables become soft.
Pour into serving bowls and spread chives on top.
Serve immediately.

Cold Cucumber Soup

Makes 4 servings

2 ½ pounds cucumber, peeled and cut into chunks
1 cup water
1 cup plain low-fat yogurt
¼ cup minced dill + 2 tablespoons chopped for garnish
3 tablespoons fresh lime juice
½ teaspoon salt

Place the cucumber and the water in a blender; blend until pureed.
Add yogurt, ¼ cup minced dill, lime juice, and salt blend fully.
Chill for 3 hours.
Transfer to a serving bowl, garnish with chopped dill, and serve with fresh bread.

Bean Soup

Makes 8 servings

⅓ cup olive oil
1 minced onion
3 garlic cloves, minced
1 celery root, peeled and cut into cubes
2 celery stems, sliced
1 carrot, peeled and sliced
1 leek, sliced
1 bay leaf
Leaves from 3 thyme stems
Leaves from 2 rosemary stems
Leaves from 10 parsley stems
Salt and freshly ground pepper
1 pound beef or lamb, cut into small cubes
2 cups white beans, soaked in cold water overnight
6 cups chicken or beef broth, or water

Put the oil in a large pot and sweat all the vegetables and herbs.
Add salt and pepper. Sweat for 10 minutes.
Add the beef and mix and sauté for 3 minutes more.
Add the beans, the broth or water, and bring to a boil.
Simmer for about 1 ½ hours until the beans are very tender.
Check seasoning and adjust taste, if necessary.
Remove the bay leaf before serving.
Serve hot with fresh French bread.

Black Bean Soup

Makes 4 servings

½ pound black beans, rinsed
1 tablespoon olive oil
1 medium-sized onion, chopped
½ green pepper, chopped
½ red pepper, chopped
1 carrot, diced
2 cloves garlic, minced
1 teaspoon sugar
1 teaspoon salt
½ teaspoon black pepper
2 bay leaves
1 teaspoon dried oregano
2 cups chicken broth
2 cups water
1 teaspoon vinegar
2 tablespoons parsley or cilantro for garnish

Put the beans in pot and cover with 2 inches water.
Cook over high heat. Bring to a boil. Cook 4 minutes.
Remove from heat and let stand for 45 minutes.
Drain and rinse beans. Set aside.
In saucepan, heat oil over medium heat. Add onion, peppers, carrot, and garlic and cook 7 minutes.
Add to mixture the sugar, salt, black pepper, bay leaf, and oregano. Cook while stirring 1 minute. Add chicken broth. Cover and simmer 10 minutes.
Add 2 cups water and beans. Cover and bring to boil.
Reduce heat to low and simmer 1½ hours until beans are tender.
Remove from heat. Stir in vinegar. Remove bay leaf from soup.
Serve hot with toasted white bread.
Garnish with parsley before serving.

Spinach Celery Soup

Makes 4 servings

1 bunch fresh spinach
2 stalks celery, thinly sliced
6 green onions, thinly sliced
1 carrot, peeled and chopped
2 tablespoons margarine
2 ½ cups water
1 cup heavy cream
2 tablespoons lemon juice
1 tablespoon chopped fresh parsley
Lemon slices for garnish

Wash and stem spinach. Chop leaves and set aside.
In saucepan, sauté celery, onions, and carrot in heated margarine for 4 minutes.
Add water. Remove from heat and chill for 30 minutes. Puree mixture in blender.
Combine pureed mixture and spinach leaves in saucepan. Bring to a boil.
Add heavy cream, reduce heat, and let simmer for 15 minutes.
Stir in lemon juice.
Before serving, sprinkle with parsley and garnish with lemon slices.

Cream of Mushroom Soup

Makes 4 servings

¼ cup butter
1 pound mushrooms, thinly sliced
2 shallots, finely chopped
1 tablespoon flour
½ teaspoon salt
¼ teaspoon white pepper
2 teaspoons tomato paste
2 cups water
1 tablespoon fresh lemon juice
1 cup half-and-half or light cream
1 cup milk, 1% fat
2 tablespoons dry vermouth

In a medium saucepan melt butter over medium heat.
Add mushrooms and shallots.
Cook and stir often until mushrooms are browned lightly and most of the liquid is gone.
Sprinkle with flour, salt, and pepper.
Add tomato paste to the mushrooms and stir gently.
Reduce heat to low and gradually blend in water.
Bring to a boil, cover and reduce heat. Simmer for 20 minutes.
Puree mushroom mixture in blender until smooth, mixing in lemon juice at the end.
Return to saucepan; blend in half-and-half and milk.
Stir often over medium heat until very hot.
Do not boil. Blend in vermouth and serve at once.

Creamed Potato Soup

Makes 4 servings

Can be served hot or cold

4 medium-sized potatoes, peeled
1 small onion, peeled
4 green onions
1 clove garlic, minced
3 tablespoons butter or margarine
3 cups water
1 cup milk, 1% or 2% fat
¾ cup heavy cream
½ teaspoon salt
¼ teaspoon white pepper
¼ teaspoon nutmeg

Garnish:
Hot soup - crisp croutons.
Cold soup - chopped green onion or parsley

Cut potatoes and onion into eighths. Coarsely chop the green onions.
In a 3-quart heavy saucepan sauté onion, green onion, and garlic in butter for 1 minute.
Add the potatoes and pour in the water.
Simmer for 20 minutes until potatoes are tender.
Puree soup in food processor or blender in batches. Transfer the pureed soup to saucepan.
Add milk, cream, salt, pepper, and nutmeg; mix well.
Chill for 3 hours if served cold. Garnish with chopped green onions or parsley.
Reheat if served hot. Serve with crisp croutons.

Cream of Carrot Soup

Makes 4 servings

If you really love carrots, this creamy, satiny soup will surprise the most ardent skeptic.

2 tablespoons butter
1 potato, peeled and thinly sliced
8 carrots, thinly sliced
1 clove garlic, chopped
½ teaspoon salt
¼ teaspoon white pepper
½ cup water
1 tablespoon flour
3 cups milk, 2% fat
1 tablespoon chopped chives
1 tablespoon chopped parsley

Place butter in a saucepan, add vegetables, garlic, salt, pepper, and water. Cover and cook until vegetables are very tender.
Stir in flour, and milk. Bring soup to a boil, reduce heat and let simmer for 20 minutes.
Puree soup mixture in blender until smooth.
Before serving add chives and parsley.
Serve hot or cold with toasted bread.

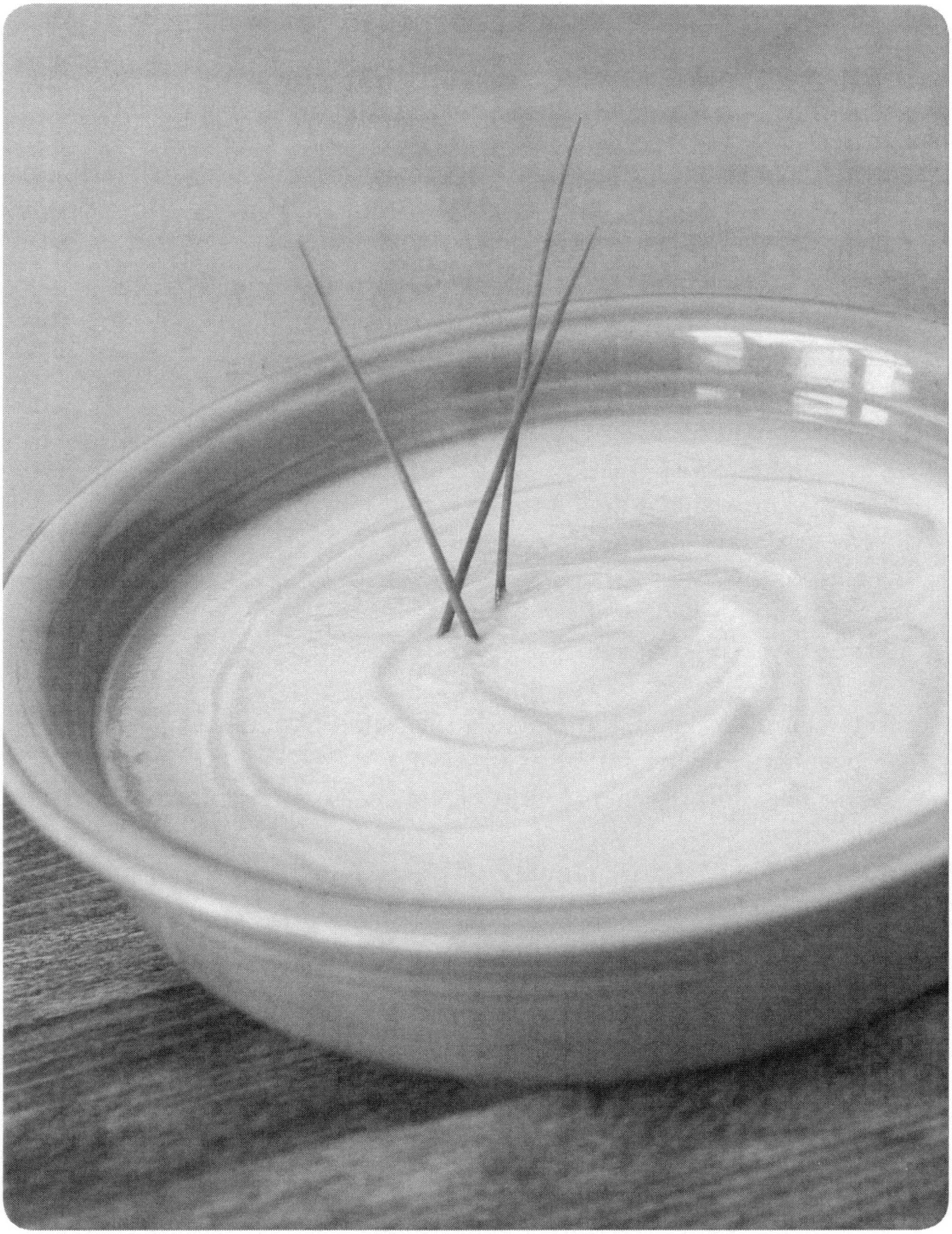

French Onion Soup

Makes 6 servings

Here's a classic I enjoy. Sometimes I'll make it without the cheese and serve it without bread to create a lighter version. Either way, this recipe is what the word "homemade" is all about!

    6 medium onions, peeled and sliced
    3 tablespoons butter
    6 cups water
    1 cup red wine
    2 cups grated Swiss cheese
    ½ teaspoon freshly grated nutmeg
    1 bay leaf
    ½ teaspoon salt
    ¼ teaspoon black pepper
    6 slices toasted French bread

In medium saucepan, sauté lightly the onion with butter.
Add water and wine and bring to a boil.
Lower heat and stir in 1 ½ cups of the cheese, nutmeg, bay leaf, salt, and pepper.
Cook over low heat 15 minutes.
Remove bay leaf from soup.

*To serve:
Place a slice of toasted bread in each of 6 bowls.
Ladle the soup over it.
Sprinkle with remaining cheese.
Serve very hot.

Potato Balls for Chicken Soup

Makes 6 servings

Based on an old Yiddish recipe, add these potato balls to a clear, flavored broth and you have a quick, tasty, light meal.

1 large uncooked potato, mashed
1 large cooked potato, mashed
1 egg white
¼ teaspoon salt
¼ teaspoon black pepper

Put all the ingredients in a bowl and mix well.
Roll small balls with your hands.
Place the balls into a boiling soup.
You may double the ingredients and freeze half of it up to 2 months.

SALAD & VEGETABLE DISHES

SALADS: PERFECT FOR A HOT DAY

Salads of all varieties, made from all types of produce, are part of the fabric of Israeli life. The summers in Israel are hot and dry. The light, cool and refreshing taste of salads is the perfect remedy.

In our family, we had salads as main dishes or side dishes to accompany our lunch or dinner. Breakfast or brunch salads were a feast for the eyes as well as the taste buds and outings with family or friends were always a showcase for the multitude of salads that Israelis love to eat.

You can serve many of the salads given here in the natural cup-shape leaves of most types of lettuce. Pick out the best leaves; they will be firm enough to easily hold the salad with dressing.

Salads are colorful with wonderful shapes and textures, ideal for special occasions and easy to prepare.

Artichoke, Peas, & Asparagus Salad

Makes 8 servings

This is a luscious recipe that can be made quite simply and will offer outstandingly delicious results.

1 pound frozen peas
1 pound artichoke hearts, fresh or frozen
2 medium onions, minced
1 tablespoon oil
1 teaspoon chicken-flavored bouillon
½ teaspoon white pepper
1 cup water
2 tablespoons minced dill
½ can asparagus (7 ounces), strained

Defrost the peas and the artichokes in the refrigerator overnight.
Sauté the onion in oil until brown.
Add the peas, the artichoke, the bouillon, the pepper, and the water.
Bring to a boil.
Lower the heat and cook for about 45 minutes.
Add the dill and the asparagus and cook for 10 additional minutes.
Serve hot.

SALADS & VEGETABLE DISHES

Colorful Spinach Salad

Makes 4 servings

A great, easy to prepare side dish that is healthy and tastes as good as it looks.

    2 tablespoons olive oil
    2 yellow peppers, thickly sliced
    1 red pepper, thickly sliced
    10 fresh thyme stems, minced
    1 pound fresh spinach leaves, rinsed and dried
    ¼ cup balsamic vinegar

Sauce:
⅓ cup olive oil
Juice from 1 lemon
1 teaspoon mustard
Salt, pepper

Simmer the oil in a frying pan. Add the peppers and cook for one minute.
Remove from heat and add the thyme. Put the spinach in a big bowl. Pour in the vinegar and stir.
Mix well all the sauce ingredients well and pour over on the spinach. Serve hot.

Lettuce Salad with Dill Sauce

Makes 6 servings

Family outings at the park are common on summer weekends and I happened to be anointed this recipe as my special picnic task. It is a particularly interesting salad that is always a welcoming site in a country that thrives on fresh vegetables.

1 head romaine lettuce
2 cucumbers cut into cubes
12 cherry tomatoes

Sauce:
4 tablespoons mayonnaise
2 tablespoons fresh lemon juice
2 tablespoons fresh dill, minced
2 tablespoons concentrated (frozen) orange juice
¼ teaspoon salt
¼ teaspoon sugar

In small bowl mix all the sauce ingredients.
Cover and refrigerate to blend flavor for 1 hour.
Wash the lettuce well and cut into big pieces.
Put the lettuce into large serving bowl.
Add the cucumber and the tomatoes. Refrigerate.
Before serving, pour the sauce on top and mix well.
Serve with toasted bread.

Radish & Apple Salad

Makes 4 servings

This is a summer dish with some pizzazz; it compliments any grilled food superbly. You can prepare it a day ahead.

½ pound white or red radishes
2 tart apples, granny smith
1 tablespoon freshly squeezed lemon juice
1 medium-sized cucumber

Dressing:
½ cup sour cream
½ cup mayonnaise
2 tablespoons fresh squeezed lemon juice
1 teaspoon dried dill weed
½ teaspoon salt
½ teaspoon sugar
2 tablespoons chopped parsley for garnish

Wash radishes and trim ends. Cut into julienne pieces.
Cut apples into eighths. Remove cores and cut into thin slices.
Toss with lemon juice to prevent darkening. Combine with radishes.
Peel cucumber and cut in half. With spoon, scoop out seeds from center. Cut into 2-inch pieces, then into julienne pieces.
Add to radishes and apples.
For dressing, stir together the sour cream, mayonnaise, lemon juice, dill weed, salt, and sugar. Before serving, mix the dressing into salad and garnish with chopped parsley.

SALADS & VEGETABLE DISHES

Cauliflower & String bean Salad

Makes 8 servings

1 head cauliflower, broken into florets only
½ pound string beans cut into 2-inch lengths
2 tablespoons chopped parsley
2 tablespoons chopped mint

Sauce:
⅓ cup olive oil
2 tablespoons fresh lemon juice
¼ teaspoon sugar
½ teaspoon salt
¼ teaspoon black pepper

Steam the cauliflower and the string beans until crispy tender.
Arrange the vegetables in a large serving platter and sprinkle the parsley on top.
In a small bowl mix all the sauce ingredients and pour over the vegetables. Sprinkle mint on top. Refrigerate to blend flavor for 3 hours. Take out of the refrigerator 20 minutes before serving.

Broccoli Salad

Makes 8 servings

2 heads fresh broccoli (stem and flowers), cut into strips lengthwise
⅓ cup olive oil
2 red peppers cut into strips
4 garlic cloves, minced
4 ounces almonds, whole or cut in halves
Salt, pepper
Juice from ½ fresh lemon

Poach the broccoli in boiling water for 2-3 minutes. Rinse with cold water and strain.
Warm up a bit of olive oil in a frying pan. Add the peppers, the garlic, and the almonds. Whip up for about 1 minute. Turn off the heat and season with salt and pepper.
Transfer the broccoli to a bowl. Season with salt and pepper.
Add the remaining olive oil and the lemon juice.
Add the contents of the frying pan and mix gently.
Serve hot.

Fresh Carrot Salad

Makes 8 servings

Prepare one day in advance.

2 pounds carrots
3 tablespoons light mayonnaise
1 teaspoon mustard
¼ teaspoon salt
Fresh juice of 1 lemon

Wash the carrots carefully and cut the ends.
Place the carrots in food processor and shred them with shredded disc.
Transfer the shredded carrots to a serving bowl and add the mayonnaise, the mustard, the salt, and the lemon juice. Mix gently.
Cover and refrigerate to blend flavor for 24 hours.
Serve cold.

Beet Salad

Makes 8 servings

Beet salad is an Israeli favorite with Shawarma, shish kebab, or any Middle Eastern food. Our family loved beets when I was a child and my husband loves beets today. I have been cooking and eating them all my life. This salad combines a subtle sweet and sour flavor with cumin and anise; both classic Indian spices. It all works well together. A low-calorie version follows.

2 pounds cooked beets
3 tablespoons vegetable oil
2 tablespoons wine vinegar
1 ½ tablespoons balsamic vinegar
1 ½ tablespoons ground cumin
1 ½ teaspoons anise seed
1 ½ teaspoons salt
1 teaspoon garlic powder
½ teaspoon sugar

Pare beets, and slice into ¼-inch slces.
Gently mix all ingredients.
Cover and refrigerate overnight to blend flavors.

Low-Calorie Beet Salad

Makes 8 servings

4 medium-sized beets
3 tablespoons vinegar
1 teaspoon sugar
4 green onions, only white part, sliced
1 tablespoon fresh parsley, minced
1 tablespoon fresh coriander, minced
¼ teaspoon salt
¼ teaspoon black pepper

Wash the beets and cook in boiling water until tender, about 30 minutes. Let cool.
Peel the beets and slice to ¼-inch thick pieces.
In a serving bowl mix all the rest of the ingredients and add the beets. Mix gently.
Cover and refrigerate to combine the flavors for 3 hours.

Cabbage Salad with Sunflower seeds

Makes 8 servings

On Friday afternoons in Israel, the shops are full of people picking up their goods for the weekend. One of my favorite shops is the one that sells only dried fruits, nuts, and seeds. Piled high in barrels would be the dates, prunes, cashews and almonds as well as sunflower and watermelon seeds. In this salad, I sprinkle some toasted sunflower and sesame seeds on the vegetables and dress it with an Asian-style sauce to add crunch and taste. The seeds are also highly nutritious and this salad is outrageously tasty and different.

½ medium-sized red cabbage, minced
2 large carrots cut into Julienne strips
2 green onion, minced
½ cup sesame seeds
½ cup sunflower seeds

Sauce:
¼ cup oil
¼ cup white vinegar
2 teaspoons sugar
2 tablespoons soy sauce

Put all the vegetables in a serving bowl. Mix well.
In a non-stick frying pan sauté the sesame seeds and the sunflower seeds without oil. Spread them on top of the vegetables.
Mix all the sauce ingredients and pour over the vegetables.
Mix well and chill to blend flavor for 2 hours.
Serve cold.

Waldorf Salad

Makes 6 servings

2 apples, granny smith, cut into small cubes
1 cup celery stems, minced
2 tablespoons fresh lemon juice
2 tablespoons chopped walnuts
¼ cup raisins
3 tablespoons light mayonnaise

In a serving bowl place all the ingredients except the mayonnaise.
Pour the mayonnaise on top and mix well.
Chill for 2 hours.
Serve cold.

Potato Salad

Makes 8 servings

2 pounds peeled potatoes
1 large onion, thinly minced
4 garlic cloves, thinly minced
½ cup olive oil
⅓ cup freshly squeezed lemon juice
Salt, freshly ground pepper
4 tablespoons thinly minced chives
4 tablespoons thinly minced parsley

Cook the potatoes in salt water until sufficiently soft. Take them out and chill them well.
Cut the potatoes into slices, ⅛ inch thick, and put them in a wide bowl. Spread the onion and the garlic on top.
Mix the oil, the lemon juice, the salt, and the pepper. Pour it all on the potatoes and mix well. Cover and refrigerate to blend flavor for 3 hours. Before serving, add the chives and the parsley. Mix and serve.
For variety, you could add anchovies to this salad.
You ought to use high-quality anchovies that were soaked in two cups of cold water for 15 minutes.
Chop up to thick pieces and add on top.

Low-Calorie Potato Salad

Makes 8 servings

This well-known dish is low fat without sacrificing taste. As a matter of fact, you may be surprised to find that it tastes even better!

4 large potatoes
2 small onions cut into small cubes
2 tablespoons parsley, minced
2 pickled cucumbers cut into small cubes
½ cup light mayonnaise
1 tablespoon mustard
2 teaspoons vinegar
½ teaspoon sugar
¾ teaspoon salt
½ teaspoon black pepper
Black olive for garnish

Cook the potatoes with the skin in salted water for 20 minutes. Cool.
Peel the potatoes and slice them into ¼-inch thick pieces.
In a large serving bowl mix the potatoes, the onions, the parsley, and the pickles.
In a small separate bowl mix the mayonnaise, mustard vinegar, sugar, and the salt and pepper and pour the mixture on top of the potatoes. Mix gently.
Cover and refrigerate to blend flavor overnight or at least 4 hours.
Garnish with olives before serving.

Cabbage Salad in Poppy Seed Sauce

Makes 8 servings

1 medium-sized cabbage, very thinly sliced
1 red pepper, very thinly sliced
1 green pepper, very thinly sliced
1 small carrot, minced
3 green onions, minced
Parsley for garnish

Sauce:
¼ cup honey
½ cup sunflower oil
5 tablespoons white wine vinegar
1 green onion
½ teaspoon salt
½ teaspoon Dijon mustard
½ teaspoon dried tarragon
2 teaspoons poppy seeds

Sauce:
Place all the ingredients in blender except for the poppy seeds and mix well.
Add the poppy seeds to the sauce.

In a large salad bowl mix all the ingredients you prepared for the salad.
Pour the sauce on top.
Garnish with parsley.

Bean Salad

Makes 12 servings

2 cups white beans
1 cup brown beans
¾ cup olive oil
¼ cup white wine vinegar
1 cup minced parsley
½ cup minced fresh basil
4 red onions, sliced
Salt and fresh ground black pepper
Sun dried tomatoes preserved in olive oil for garnish

Soak beans in water overnight. Rinse and transfer to a large pot and cover the beans with water.
Cover the pot and cook until the beans turn tender. Strain and chill.
Transfer to a large serving bowl, add the rest of ingredients and mix well.
Cover and refrigerate to blend flavor for 3 hours.
Garnish with sun-dried tomatoes before serving.
Serve moderately cold.

Zucchini & Squash Salad

Makes 8 servings

My nephew demanded zucchini every day for dinner, so my sister and I decided to vary its preparation to keep things less boring. This salad is the result. After eating the zucchini mixed with carrots and squash, he never ate zucchini alone again.

Can be served cold or hot.

2 ½ tablespoons vegetable oil
3 medium-sized carrots
4 small zucchini
4 small yellow squash
1 tablespoon dried basil
Salt and pepper
Fresh basil leaves for garnish

Cut the vegetables into julienne strips.
Heat the oil in a large skillet and sauté the carrots for 1 to 2 minutes.
Add the zucchini and the squash and cook for 3 to 5 minutes until tender-crisp.
Add the basil, salt and pepper; then mix.
To serve cold, transfer the salad to a serving bowl, cover and chill for 3 hours, sprinkle with chopped basil and serve with fresh whole wheat bread.
To serve hot, transfer the salad to a serving bowl, sprinkle chopped fresh basil, and serve with toasted bread.

String Beans with Tomatoes

Makes 4 servings

1 pound string beans, stems trimmed
1 cup chopped ripe tomatoes
2 tablespoons fresh marjoram leaves, chopped
1 tablespoon olive oil
Salt and freshly ground pepper

In medium-sized pan combine beans, tomatoes, and chopped marjoram leaves.
Cover and bring to a boil over high heat.
Reduce heat; simmer until beans are tender-crisp, 5–7 minutes.
Stir in oil. Add salt and pepper to taste.
Serve hot.

Zucchini with Walnuts

Makes 6 servings

Nuts grow abundantly and are native to Israel; we use them often in our cooking and everyday snacks. This salad combination not only creates an elegant dish, but it adds a distinctive, lively taste to this popular vegetable,

1 ½ pounds zucchini
⅓ cup olive oil
4 green onions, sliced
⅓ cup dry white wine
3 tablespoons fresh lemon juice
⅓ cup water
1 cup chopped walnuts

Wash the zucchini and cut off ends. Cut into ½-inch slices. (It needs no peeling.)
In skillet heat olive oil and sauté zucchini and green onions for 6 minutes, stirring frequently.
Pour in wine, lemon juice, and water. Simmer for 7 minutes longer.
Toast nuts at 325° for 6 minutes, stirring frequently.
Stir nuts into skillet and mix gently.
Serve hot with broiled or baked fish.

Coleslaw Salad

Makes 4 servings

4 cups finely chopped cabbage
½ cup chopped red pepper
½ cup chopped green pepper
¼ cup unpeeled, seeded, and diced cucumber

Dressing:
½ cup sour cream
½ cup milk
2 tablespoons fresh squeezed lemon Juice
1 tablespoon chopped green onion
1 tablespoon chopped parsley
1 clove garlic
1 teaspoon salt

In large bowl, combine cabbage, red and green pepper, and cucumber.
Prepare dressing by placing all ingredients in blender and process until pureed. If the mixture is too thick, stir in more milk.
Pour dressing over the vegetables, tossing well.
Serve very cold.

Mashed Potatoes

Makes 6 servings

1 ½ pounds potatoes, peeled and quartered
½ cup water
1 tablespoon margarine
1 cup finely chopped onions
2 cloves garlic, minced
⅓ cup non-dairy sour cream
¼ teaspoon black pepper

Put potatoes in a saucepan with water, cover and bring to boil.
Cook 15 minutes, until tender.
In nonstick skillet, melt margarine over medium heat, add onion and garlic and cook for 4 minutes.
Drain cooked potatoes and mash with water and the non-dairy sour cream. Stir in onion mixture and black pepper.
To serve hot place potato mixture on serving platter and pour meat or lamb stew over top.
Serve cold as a salad.

MAIN DISHES

POULTRY

Chicken with Garlic Cloves

Makes 4 servings

The great taste of this simple dish is enhanced by the health benefits of garlic.

1 chicken, quartered, skinned, or 4 chicken legs with thighs, cut in half
½ teaspoon salt
½ teaspoon freshly ground black pepper
⅓ cup olive oil
3 fresh thyme stems
2 fresh rosemary stems
24 whole garlic cloves, unpeeled
12 small potatoes, peeled and cut into quarters
1 cup dry white wine
2 ounces soft margarine, cut into small squares

Put salt and pepper on the chicken. Warm up the oil in a large saucepan. When hot, fry the chicken parts until they turn brownish.
Add thyme, rosemary, and garlic. Fry for 5 minutes, stirring intermittently. Add potatoes and mix. Add the wine and bring to a boil.
Heat up the oven at 350° Transfer the contents in the saucepan to a baking pan and spread the margarine squares on top.
Cover with aluminum foil and bake for 45 minutes to an hour. From time to time, turn the chicken, and pour the liquids from the bottom of the pan on the chicken.
Serve immediately with green salad.

Chicken Cutlets in Peach Sauce

Makes 6 servings

While this recipe might demand you to be a bit more meticulous with its preparation, the results are well worth the effort and extra time.

2 pounds ground chicken (breast and leg)
2 large onions, thinly minced
3 garlic cloves, chopped
3 tablespoons bread crumbs
½ cup parsley, minced
1 slice white bread, soaked in water, squeezed, and crumbled
2 eggs
1 teaspoon salt
1 teaspoon black pepper
Oil for sauté

Sauce:
2 onions, thinly minced
4 garlic cloves, chopped
½ cup soy sauce
3 tablespoons citrus vinegar
3 tablespoons sugar, or artificial sweetener
2 tablespoons corn flour
1 cup water
1 29-ounce can half peaches preserved in syrup

Put the chicken meat in a large bowl; add the onion, the garlic, the bread crumbs, the parsley, the bread, the eggs, the salt, and pepper and mix well. Make small balls from the mix (about 1 inch), sauté the balls in a bit of oil and put aside.

Sauce:

Sauté the onions in a medium-sized pot until golden brown.

Add the garlic, the soy sauce, the vinegar, and the sugar. Mix the corn flour in a cup of water and add to the pot while mixing.

Cut the peaches into ¼-inch cubes. Add the peaches with the syrup to the pot. Bring to a boil.

Put the cutlets in the pot. Lower the heat and cook 10 minutes, until the cutlets are well soaked in the sauce.

Serve hot over white rice.

Chicken with Wine & Balsamic Vinegar

Makes 4 servings

Here is an excellent entrée that is wonderfully tasty, and not at all hard to make.

⅓ cup oil olive
1 large onion, sliced
2 garlic cloves, peeled and sliced
1 carrot, sliced
2 celery stem, sliced
1 bay leaf
4 chicken legs with thighs cut in halves
½ teaspoon salt
¼ teaspoon freshly crushed black pepper
1 tablespoon freshly minced tarragon, or ½ tablespoon dried tarragon
2 tablespoons balsamic vinegar
½ cup dry white wine

Put the oil in a pot and steam the onion, the garlic, the carrot, the celery, and the bay leaf for 5 minutes, until the vegetables turn tender.
Put the salt and pepper on the chicken. Pour some oil in a frying pan and fry the chicken on both sides until brown. Add the chicken to the pot together with the vegetables and mix.
Add the tarragon and vinegar. Add some salt and pepper and cook for 5 minutes.
Add the wine, bring to a boil, and cook in a covered pot on a low heat for 45 minutes.
Discard the bay leaf before serving.
Serve over white rice.

Chicken Legs in Honey Sauce

Makes 6 servings

It is traditional on the Jewish New Year to cook something with honey to symbolize the sweetness of life in the coming year. I created this holiday meal with an Asian twist, combining soy sauce, honey, and red wine into a pleasantly mild sweet and sour sauce. The results will be supremely rewarding.

6 chicken legs with thighs
3 tablespoons soy sauce
4 tablespoons honey
3 teaspoons garlic powder
4 tablespoons semi-dry red wine
¼ tablespoon cumin
1 packet chicken-flavored bouillon
1 cup boiling water
Salt and pepper

Arrange the chicken side by side in a baking pan.
Mix all the other ingredients, except the water, in a separate bowl.
While stirring the mix, slowly add the boiling water.
Pour the sauce on the chicken.
Bake in the oven at 375° for 45 minutes.
Lower the temperature to 300° and bake for another 15 to 20 minutes.
Serve immediately with roasted potatoes.
You may freeze the baked chicken up to 3 weeks, and warm up each piece in a microwave.

Chicken Breast in Oranges

Makes 8 servings

In Israel, the oranges are lush, juicy and sweet. I remember making this dish using full, ripe Israeli oranges and the combination was heavenly. The orange sauce also adds good moisture to the chicken breast.

4 whole chicken breasts, split, boned, and skinned
½ cup freshly squeezed orange juice
2 fresh tarragon stems, minced
3 garlic cloves, minced

Sauce:
2 cups chicken stock or 1 cube chicken-flavored bouillon,
    mixed with 2 cups boiling water
½ cup freshly squeezed orange juice
2 tablespoons corn flour
½ cup water
1 stem fresh tarragon leaves, minced
½ teaspoon salt
¼ teaspoon black pepper

Place the chicken pieces in a bowl. Mix the orange juice, the tarragon, and the garlic. Pour on top of the chicken. Refrigerate overnight, or at least for 4 hours.

Sauce:
Boil the stock and the juice. Dilute the corn flour in ½ cup water. Add to the boiling liquid and cook until the liquid becomes thick. Add the tarragon leaves, the salt and the pepper. Add the chicken to the boiling liquid and cook for 5 minutes.
Take the chicken pieces out of the sauce. Arrange on a serving platter. Serve the sauce separately.

Chicken Breast Roll in Wine Sauce

Makes 8 servings

I love cooking with wine. The richness of the liver is perfectly complimented by the asparagus and wine in this dish. Choose a fine white wine and the flavor of the grape will be absorbed by the chicken, adding an extra dimension of complexity and fullness to this dish.

- 8 chicken livers
- 2 tablespoons oil for sauté
- 2 large onions cut into strips
- Fresh asparagus bunch or 14-ounce asparagus can
- 4 whole chicken breasts, split, boned, and skinned
- 2 cups dry white wine
- 1 packet chicken-flavored bouillon
- Freshly ground black pepper
- Olive oil

In a frying pan, sauté the chicken livers in a bit of oil. Take out and cut into thin pieces.

Sauté the onions with 2 tablespoons oil until they turn golden. Cook the asparagus in salt water 4 minutes. Strain and cut every stem into 3 parts. If you use canned asparagus, strain and cut into 3 parts.

Flatten all the chicken breasts. Put them on a flat surface.

On each breast, at the end, put one liver, a few asparagus stems and some of the sautéed onion, and fold into a roll shape.

Put the chicken rolls in a baking pan lubricated with a bit of olive oil with their open side facing down.

Spread on top the remainder of the asparagus and the onion.

In a small pot, put the wine, the bouillon, and the pepper.

Bring to a boil. Pour into the pan with the chicken. Cover with aluminum foil, and bake at 350° for 20 minutes.

Serve hot with linguini.

Chicken Breasts in Lemon & Capers

Makes 4 servings

A distinctively tasty chicken dish that is easy to prepare and simple to make.

2 whole chicken breasts, split, boned, and skinned
⅓ cup flour
¼ teaspoon black pepper
½ teaspoon paprika
1 ½ tablespoons oil
¼ cup chicken broth or water
2 tablespoons fresh lemon juice
2 tablespoons capers, drained

On a flat surface pound each piece of chicken to ¼-inch thickness.
Combine the flour, the pepper, and the paprika on a plate.
Press the chicken breasts into the mixture, coating them evenly on each side and shaking off any excess mixture.
In a heavy skillet heat the oil and sauté the chicken breasts over medium heat, 3 minutes on each side.
Transfer the chicken to a heated platter.
Add the chicken broth to the skillet, stir in the lemon juice and the capers, and heat through. Transfer the chicken to 4 serving plates, and pour the sauce over the chicken.
Serve with linguini.

Chicken in Orange Juice & Kumquat

Makes 4 servings

1 chicken, skinned and cut into 8 pieces
8 whole kumquats, or 1 orange, peeled and cut into 8 pieces
2 tablespoons olive oil
Salt and pepper

Marinade:
2 cups fresh-squeezed orange juice
⅓ cup olive oil
1 onion, thinly sliced
3 garlic cloves, minced
2 teaspoons fresh lemon juice

Mix all the marinade ingredients.
Marinate all the chicken pieces overnight, or at least 4 hours.
Take the chicken out and dry it well.
In a large saucepan, sauté the chicken pieces until golden brown. Set aside.
Strain the marinade and bring the liquids to a boil until it thickens on low heat.
Sauté the onion and the garlic in a saucepan in which you fried the chicken pieces.
Cook the kumquat or the oranges in boiling water for 20 minutes and take them out.
Put the chicken back into the saucepan.
Pour over the thickened sauce along with the kumquat or orange pieces over the chicken.
Add salt and pepper. Cook covered for 30 minutes on a medium heat.
And uncovered for 15 minutes more.
Serve immediately over white rice.

POULTRY

Chicken in Mustard

Makes 4 servings

2 ounces margarine
1 large onion, minced
2 garlic cloves, minced
4 chicken legs and thighs, split in 2 and skinned
½ cup dry white wine
3 tablespoons Dijon mustard
2 tablespoons olive oil
Salt and freshly ground black pepper
3 tablespoons parsley, finely minced

Put the margarine in a large pot and steam the onion and the garlic. Add the chicken pieces and sauté until brownish all around. Add the wine and cook on a high heat until most of the wine evaporates.
Mix the mustard, the oil, the salt and the pepper, and add into the pot. Bring to a boil and cook on low heat for 45 minutes.
Add the parsley and mix.
Serve hot over white rice.

Ginger Chicken

Makes 4 servings

3 tablespoons teriyaki sauce
1 tablespoon vegetable oil
2 teaspoons grated fresh ginger
2 tablespoons fresh orange juice
4 chicken legs and thighs, split, boned, and skinned
¼ teaspoon orange zest

In large bowl, mix teriyaki sauce, oil, ginger, and juice.
Add chicken to mixture and marinate for 10 minutes.
Preheat broiler. Remove chicken from marinade. Put marinade aside.
On broiler pan rack, put chicken and broil 8 minutes.
Turn the chicken and broil 5 minutes.
Transfer to plate and keep warm. In skillet, bring marinade to a boil.
Add orange zest and remove from heat.
Pour marinade over chicken.
Serve hot with noodles.

Chicken Breast Filled With Mushrooms

Makes 4 servings

The mushrooms add a lovely, smoked woodsy flavor to the chicken that will satisfy the most demanding connoisseur. I love to use mushrooms because they elevate a dish with their elegant, deep flavor.

2 whole chicken breasts, split, boned, and skinned
2 tablespoons flour
2 eggs, beaten
Bread crumbs
2 tablespoons olive oil

For the Stuffing:
1 tablespoon margarine
1 onion, diced
1 pound fresh mushrooms, sliced
3 tablespoons dry white wine
¼ teaspoon nutmeg
Leaves from 2 fresh thyme stems
½ teaspoon salt
¼ teaspoon black pepper

Open deep pockets in the chicken breast pieces in order to fill them later.

Stuffing Preparation:
Melt the margarine in a frying pan.
Sauté the onion until brown golden.
Add the mushrooms and the wine. Sauté until the liquids evaporate.
Season with nutmeg, thyme leavs, salt, and pepper. Remove from heat and chill.
Fill the pockets in the chicken pieces with the stuffing.
Dip in the flour, the eggs, and the bread crumbs.
Sauté in oil on both sides, about 2 minutes for each side, until the pieces turn golden brown.
Serve the chicken breasts on a bed of steamed vegetables.

Chicken Baked in Sesame

Makes 4 servings

Very quick preparation

1 egg
2 tablespoons soy sauce
1 cup bread crumbs
½ cup sesame seeds
½ teaspoon, ginger powder
4 chicken legs and thighs, cut in halves, boned, and skinned
2 ounces margarine, melted
½ lemon, sliced

Preheat the oven to 400°.
In a bowl, beat the egg with the soy sauce.
In another bowl, mix the bread crumbs, the sesame, and the ginger powder.
Dip the chicken pieces in the egg mixture and then in the breadcrumb mixture. Place the chicken in a baking pan. Spread on top melted margarine.
Bake 30 minutes until brown golden.
Serve hot with sliced lemon.

BEEF

Roast Beef Glazed in Orange

Makes 4 servings

Israelis have come up with some very creative uses for oranges in their cuisine. In this dish, which I prepare for the high holidays, the orange glaze with elements of sweet, sour, and spice added to the meat creates a rich and wonderfully complex taste. Garnish the roast with orange segments for an attractive presentation. You will surely make many friends with this dish.

¾ cup brown sugar
2 tablespoons orange juice
1 ½ tablespoons lemon juice
5 tablespoons oil
1 teaspoon ginger powder or 1 tablespoon fresh ginger, thinly scraped
½ teaspoon mustard
½ teaspoon salt
¼ teaspoon freshly ground black pepper
2 ½ pounds beef for roasting (all in one piece)
1 orange, sliced but not peeled for garnish

Preheat oven to 450°.
Mix the sugar, the fruit juices, the oil, the ginger, the mustard, the salt, and black pepper.
Smear this glaze all around the piece of beef.
Lubricate a baking pan with oil and place the piece of beef in it.
Put into the oven and roast for 20 minutes.
Lower the temperature to a 250°. and continue to roast for another 1 ½ hours.
During this time, baste the beef at least 4 times in the sauce that has been accumulated in the pan. Transfer beef to a serving platter and garnish with orange slices.
Serve hot with roasted potatoes.
You can spread some margarine on the orange slices and grill until they become golden brown.

Beef Chunk Cooked in Red Wine

Makes 8 servings

Here is a holiday meal that uses many interesting ingredients, takes a little more time to make, but ultimately the results will be supremely rewarding.

You may prepare it one or two days in advance and warm it up 20 minutes before serving.

5 pounds beef, tied with butcher's twine in the shape of a roll
6 fresh thyme stems
3 fresh rosemary stems
Salt and freshly ground black pepper
¼ cup olive oil
3 sliced celery stems, sliced
3 large onions, sliced
6 garlic cloves, peeled and sliced
4 ounces fresh mushrooms, sliced
4 bones with the marrow, (optional)
¼ cup soy sauce
4 cups red wine or 2 cups red wine and 2 cups beef stock

Weave into the twine that wraps the beef 4 thyme stems and 2 rosemary stems. Sprinkle salt and pepper on the beef. Warm up the oil in a large pot that will comfortably hold the beef.
When the oil is hot, put the beef in the pot carefully and sear it all over for 10 minutes until it becomes brown.
Take the beef out of the pot.
Put the cut-up vegetables and the remaining thyme and rosemary leaves into the pot and gently cook them for about 5 minutes.
Add the bones, soy sauce, wine and salt and pepper. Bring to a boil and cook for 10 minutes.
Put the meat back in the pot and cook on low heat for 1 hour and 45 minutes.

At this point you may prepare one or two days in advance and proceed to warm it up 30 minutes on medium heat before serving.

Take the meat out of the pot, strain the vegetables from the liquids, and put the liquids back in the pot.

Cook the liquids until it thickens, about 1 cup. Check and adjust the seasoning.

Slice the beef, and transfer to a large serving platter. Pour the sauce on top.

Serve with the cooked vegetables.

Beef Casserole with Quinces & Dried Fruits

Makes 8 servings

Quinces, which come out in the fall, are a yellow, apple-like fruit with a rough skin. It is dry and hard like wood and therefore somewhat difficult to cut. However, it softens up when cooked thereby adding lots of wonderful flavor. This traditional holiday dish, which combines meat with quince and dried fruit, will bring forth a dish both dramatic in flavor and presentation.

4 cups beef stock or water
2 ½ pounds lean beef, cut into 1-inch cubes
5 quinces cut to quarters
8 ounces dried apricots
8 ounces dried, pitted prunes
8 ounces dried, pitted dates
1 cup fresh orange juice
6 medium-sized tomatoes cut into small cubes
2 tablespoons tomato paste
¼ cup oil
½ teaspoon salt
¼ teaspoon black pepper

Boil the beef stock or the water in a large pot. Add the meat and cook for 45 minutes.
In a skillet, sauté the quinces in a bit of oil for 2 minutes and add to the pot.
Add the rest of the ingredients to the pot and bring to a boil.
Lower the heat and cook for 1 hour, or until the meat is tender and most of the liquid is evaporated.
Serve immediately over white rice.

Burgers in Pineapple Sauce

Makes 4 servings

We have come a long way from burgers and ketchup on a bun, leaping here into something different, delightful, and special.

- 1 pound ground beef
- 2 tablespoons light soy sauce
- 1 tablespoon oil
- 1 medium onion, sliced lengthwise
- 2 teaspoons minced ginger root
- 1 cup water
- 1 small cauliflower, or 1 small broccoli floweret
- 1 8-ounce can pineapple in syrup
- 2 tablespoons cornstarch
- 1 medium green pepper cut in rings
- 2 cups cooked white rice

Mix ground beef and 1 tablespoon soy sauce.
Shape meat in 4 large patties, ½-inch thick.
In medium skillet heat oil, add patties, and brown quickly on both sides. Remove meat from skillet.
Add onion and ginger and sauté lightly.
Return patties to skillet. Add water and cauliflower or broccoli.
Cover and cook 3 minutes until burgers are cooked to your desire. Remove from skillet.
Drain pineapple, reserving ½ cup syrup. Dice pineapple.
Blend cornstarch, pineapple syrup, and remaining 1 tablespoons soy sauce.
Stir mixture into skillet. Cook, stirring until slightly thickened.
Return burgers to skillet and reheat.
Arrange green pepper rings over rice.
Place burgers on top. Spoon the sauce over.

BEEF

Goulash with Green Pepper

Makes 4 servings

This classic Hungarian dish should be spicy. My mom used to make it quite often.

1 ½ pounds boneless beef chuck
2 tablespoons olive oil
2 medium-sized onion, chopped
½ cup red wine
1 ½ tablespoons sweet paprika
1 teaspoon salt
1 green pepper, cut into ½-inch cubes
1 green hot pepper, sliced

Cut beef into 1 ½ inch cubes.
In saucepan, sauté the beef with oil over medium to high heat. Brown slowly until richly browned on all sides.
Add the onions and cook 3 minutes until onions are softened.
Add the red wine, paprika, salt, and peppers, blend well.
Cover and cook on medium heat without allowing boiling, for 2 hours, until meat is tender, but not soft. Add more water if needed.
Serve over cooked potatoes or white rice.

Ground Beef Vegetable Casserole

Makes 4 servings

1 tablespoon oil
1 pound lean ground beef
2 large onion, chopped
3 stalks celery, sliced
1 parsnip, peeled, cut julienne
2 large carrots, cut julienne
1 small head Chinese cabbage, sliced
2 cups beef broth or 2 cups water and 2 packets beef flavor bouillon
⅓ cup uncooked rice
1 teaspoon salt
½ teaspoon dried oregano leaves
2 tablespoons chopped parsley for garnish

In heavy pot put oil, beef, and onion. Brown over medium heat while stirring.
Add celery, parsnip, carrots, and cabbage. Cook 5 minutes until meat is no longer pink and vegetables begin to get tender.
Add broth or water and beef flavor bouillon, rice, salt, and oregano. Stir. Cover and simmer for 20 minutes.
Garnish with parsley before serving.
Serve with fresh whole wheat bread.
You may add or substitute vegetables such as broccoli, potatoes, peas, or cauliflower.

Beef Stew with Red Wine

Makes 6 servings

Prepare a day in advance.

My family always requests that I prepare the beef stew when visiting Israel on holidays. While Beef Stew may not appear in any way out of the ordinary, my recipe stands out most notably for its liberal use of red wine and herbs. Equally as important, it can be prepared a day or two in advance while still retaining all or even more of its original flavors! This dish is equally suitable for entertaining as well as for special occasions.

3 ½ - 4 pounds beef for roasting
2 ounces margarine
2 tablespoons flour
4 ounces smoked meat, cut into strips (optional)
Sauce:
3 cups semi-dry red wine
1 carrot, peeled and sliced
2 celery stems, sliced
2 large onions, minced
6 garlic cloves, sliced
6 fresh thyme stems
2 bay leaves

Cut the meat into 1-inch cubes.
In a pot, mix the sauce ingredients. Bring to a boil. Cook 10 minutes and cool.
Put the meat cubes in the sauce mix. Refrigerate overnight, or at least for 4 hours. Strain the meat and dry well. Keep the sauce ingredients aside.
In a large pot, simmer the margarine and sauté the meat cubes on all sides until somewhat brown. Add the flour and the smoked meat. Mix and sauté for another minute.
Strain the sauce ingredients and add to the pot. Bring to a boil.
Lower the heat and cook for 2 hours.

At this stage the sauce has to be thick. If the sauce is not thick enough, take the meat out of the pot, reduce the sauce, put the meat back in the pot, and mix.

Discard the bay leaves.

Serve hot with potatoes.

Green Pepper Steak

Makes 4 servings

When I first made Green Pepper Steak for my husband, he proclaimed, "Did you order this from a restaurant?" This recipe is a testimonial of how good a dish can taste when simple ingredients are combined with good, old-fashioned love and some imagination!

    1 pound beef chuck or round
    ¼ cup soy sauce
    1 clove garlic
    1 teaspoon ground ginger
    ¼ cup vegetable oil
    1 cup green onion, thinly sliced
    1 cup red pepper, cut into 1-inch squares
    2 stalks celery, thinly sliced
    2 tomatoes, cut into wedges
    1 tablespoon cornstarch
    1 cup water

With a very sharp knife, cut beef across grain into thin strips, ⅛ inch thick.
In large bowl combine soy sauce, garlic, and ginger. Add beef. Toss and set aside.
In large frying pan or wok, heat oil. Add beef and toss over high heat until browned. Cover and simmer for 30 minutes over low heat.
Turn heat up and add onion, pepper and celery. Toss until vegetables are tender crisp, about 10 minutes.
Mix cornstarch with water. Add to pan. Stir and cook until thickened. Add tomatoes and heat through.
Serve over white rice.

Meat Loaf

Makes 10 servings

This non-traditional meatloaf is one of my personal specialties! It requires no sauce, as the taste is so moist and delicate you would think you are biting into butter! The recipe is quick and its supreme seasoning and ingredients lends itself to making and preserving larger quantities over longer periods of time. My family virtually demands this dish when visiting the States! (If you do freeze a portion, do so unbaked).

In a 4 ½ x 8 ½-inch loaf pan:
1 medium-sized onion, finely chopped
½ green pepper, finely chopped
½ cup tomato sauce, or 2 tablespoon tomato paste
    and 2 tablespoon water
2 beaten eggs or 1 whole egg and 2 egg whites
2 slices of dark bread soaked in water, drained and crumbled
½ teaspoons dry thyme
1 teaspoon salt
½ teaspoon black pepper
2 pounds ground beef

Preheat the oven to 350 °.
In a saucepan, cook the onion and the green pepper in boiling water until tender.
Transfer the onion mixture to a large bowl. Stir in the tomato sauce, the eggs, the bread, the thyme, the salt, and the pepper. Stir well.
Add the ground beef and mix well.
Pour the mixture into loaf pan cover with aluminum foil and bake for 1 ¼ hours.
Let cool for 10 minutes. Transfer to a long platter, slice and serve.

Bean Stew with Red Meat

Makes 8 servings

1 large onion
6 garlic cloves
3 large carrots
3 celery stems
2 tablespoons olive oil
2 pounds beef, cut into 2-inches pieces
2 cups white beans, soaked in water overnight
3 cups dry red wine
2-3 bones with the marrow
6 thyme stems, leaves only
2 bay leaf
½ teaspoon salt
¼ teaspoon ground black pepper
2 cups water
2 tablespoons minced parsley for garnish

Peel the onion, the garlic, the carrots, and cut into ½-inch pieces. Slice the celery.
In a large saucepan, sauté the vegetables in oil on a high heat until the vegetables turn somewhat golden brown. Add the beef pieces and sauté while mixing until the pieces sear all around.
Add the soaked beans, the wine, the bones, the thyme leaves, bay leaf, the salt, the black pepper, and the water. Bring to a boil and cook while covered on a low heat for 2 hours.
Remove the bay leaf before serving and garnish with parsley.
Serve hot.

LAMB

Lamb Stew with Black Olives

Makes 6 servings

If you are a lamb lover, this stew will knock you over. The sharpness of the olives cuts into the fat of the lamb, which ultimately enhances the taste of the meat. The results are a stew that stands out way beyond the ordinary! It is also simple to prepare. Trimming the excess fat keeps the diet intact.

3 tablespoons olive oil
2 large onions, minced
3 cloves garlic, minced
3 pounds lamb, cut into 1-inch cubes
1 ½ cup dry white wine
1 tomato, cut into small cubes
1 cup water
2 tablespoons minced fresh rosemary
½ teaspoon salt
¼ teaspoon black pepper
½ pound pitted black olive, cut into strips
3 potatoes, peeled and cut into 1-inch cubes
2 tablespoons minced parsley

In a large pot, sauté with oil the onion and the garlic.
Add the meat, and sauté for 3 minutes until the meat turns brown.
Add the wine, the tomatoes, the water, the rosemary, the salt and the pepper. Bring to a boil.
Continue to cook on a low heat 25 minutes. Add the olive, the potatoes, and the parsley.
Cover and cook on low heat for 40 minutes.
Serve hot over white rice.

Lamb with Herbs

Makes 4 servings

2 tablespoons margarine
1 tablespoon vegetable oil
4 pieces boneless lamb chops, (8 ounces each)
½ teaspoon salt
¼ teaspoon freshly ground black pepper
3 shallots or medium size onion, chopped
3 fresh thyme stems, chopped
¾ cup dry red wine
2 teaspoons Dijon mustard
2 fresh thyme stems, chopped for garnish

In a large skillet, melt the margarine over medium heat, add the oil and braise the lamb pieces on both sides for 8 to 10 minutes.
Season with salt and pepper, remove from skillet, and keep in warm place.
Remove the excess fat from saucepan.
In the same skillet sauté the shallots and simmer with thyme.
Add the wine and the mustard and simmer on a low heat.
Reduce the sauce by half.
Slice the lamb, transfer to a serving platter, spoon the sauce on top, and garnish with the chopped thyme.
Serve over white rice.

Lamb in Orange

Makes 8 servings

2 small oranges
8 slices boneless lamb (8 ounces each)
4 tablespoons flour
2 tablespoons vegetable oil
½ teaspoon salt
¼ teaspoon black pepper
2 garlic cloves, minced
½ cup dry white wine
3 tablespoons concentrated orange juice (frozen)
2 tablespoons peppercorns

Preheat the oven to 375°.
Peel the oranges, cut into wedges, and set aside.
Coat the lamb pieces with 2 tablespoons flour.
Heat the oil in an ovenproof large saucepan and cook both sides of the lamb over a medium heat for 10 minutes.
Season with salt, pepper and minced garlic.
Transfer the saucepan to the preheated oven and cook for 15 minutes.
Remove the saucepan from oven, transfer the lamb to a large platter, cover with aluminum foil, and set aside.
Remove the excess fat from the saucepan.
Add the wine, the orange juice, the peppercorn, and the remaining 2 tablespoons of flour.
Cook over medium heat until sauce is reduced by half.
Cut the lamb fillets in ½-inch slices.
Place on a serving platter and garnish with orange wedges.
Serve with white rice.

Lamb Vegetable Stew

Makes 6 servings

1 ½ tablespoons vegetable oil
1 ½ pounds leg of lamb, cut into 1-inch cubes
3 tablespoons flour
3 cloves garlic, minced
1 ½ cups leeks, white and green parts, sliced
1 cup carrots, sliced
1 cup green pepper, chopped
1 cup onion, chopped
1 cup mushrooms, sliced
½ cup zucchini, sliced
2 tablespoons tomato paste
1 cup dry red wine
2 cups tomatoes, chopped
1 cube beef-flavored bouillon
1 ½ cups water
1 tablespoon dried rosemary
1 tablespoon dried thyme
½ tsp black pepper
2 bay leaves

In large saucepan, heat 1 tablespoon oil over medium-high heat. Dust the lamb cubes in the flour and add to the saucepan. Cook for 5 minutes. Remove lamb from saucepan.
In same saucepan, heat remaining ½ tablespoon oil over medium heat. Add garlic, leeks, carrots, peppers, onions, mushrooms, and zucchini. Cook 10 minutes, stirring occasionally.
Stir in tomato paste and wine.
Return lamb to saucepan along with tomatoes.
Dissolve beef bouillon cube in 2 tablespoons hot water, add to saucepan.
Add water, rosemary, thyme, black pepper, and bay leaf. Bring to a boil, cover, and simmer 45 minutes over medium-low heat. Discard the bay leaves.
Serve with potatoes.

VEAL

Roasted Veal with Prune

Makes 8 servings

The lovely, tender veal is matched with the elegance of dried prunes. A perfect meal for the whole family and to serve on festive occasions.

¼ cup oil
8 cloves garlic, peeled
2 bay leaves
3 pounds boneless veal, rolled and tied

Sauce:
½ pound prunes, soaked in cold water overnight
2 teaspoons soy sauce
2 teaspoons chicken or beef bouillon
2 teaspoons brown sugar (optional)
1 teaspoon black pepper

In large saucepan, heat the oil, add the garlic, the bay leaves, and the veal roll, Sauté the meat on both sides for 10 minutes.
Continue to cook on low heat with the pot covered for 1 hour.
Pre-heat the oven to 350 °.
Take the veal out of saucepan, slice it in half and place both pieces into large baking pan.
Mix the liquid from saucepan, the prunes with the soaked water, the soy sauce, the bouillon, the sugar, and the pepper; then pour over the sliced veal.
Cover with aluminum foil and bake for 2 hours.
Take out of the oven and discard the bay leaves.
Transfer the veal to a large, long platter and slice the meat.
Put the prunes between slices and pour the sauce from pan over the top.
Serve with white rice.

Veal Stew with Mustard & Honey

Makes 6 servings

Honey, mustard, and veal combine for a different, yet wonderfully enticing dish.

6 tablespoons olive oil
4 scallions, minced, the white part only
2 garlic cloves, minced
3 pounds veal, cut up into 1-inch cubes
½ teaspoon salt
¼ teaspoon black pepper
1 ½ cup dry red wine
3 tablespoons mustard
6 tablespoons honey
1 tablespoon balsamic vinegar
6 fresh tarragon leaves, minced
2 tablespoons raisins

Warm up the oil in a large pot and sauté the scallions and the garlic for 3 minutes.
Add the veal pieces and sauté until brown all around.
Add the wine, the salt, and the pepper. Bring to a boil. Lower the heat. Cover and cook for 45 minutes.
In a small bowl, mix the mustard, the honey, and the vinegar.
Add to the pot and cook another 25 minutes.
Toward the end of cooking, add the tarragon leaves and mix well.
Before serving, spread raisins on the dish and serve.
Serve hot, over white rice.

Veal Shoulder with Mushrooms

Makes 4 servings

1 ½ pounds boneless veal shoulder
3 ounces margarine
¼ cup brandy or cognac
1 teaspoon Dijon mustard
2 ½ cups chicken broth
½ cup dry white wine
1 tablespoon currant jelly
¼ cup chopped parsley
1 teaspoon dried tarragon leaves
½ teaspoon dried sage
1 tablespoon cornstarch
½ pound fresh mushrooms
1 cup green pitted olives

Cut meat into 2-inches cubes.
In wide frying pan, melt 2 ounces of margarine and brown meat.
When all the pieces are browned, add brandy to ignite the flame. Stir in mustard.
Transfer meat to a large casserole with lid.
Pour in chicken broth and wine.
Cover with aluminum foil and place in oven. Cook at 325° for 2 hours until veal is very tender.
Add jelly, half of the parsley, tarragon, and sage.
Mix cornstarch with 1 tablespoon water and stir into casserole.
Cook until thickened.
Melt remaining margarine in frying pan and brown mushrooms over high heat for 3 minutes.
When ready to serve, gannish with mushrooms, olives, and the remaining parsley.
Serve with fresh whole grain bread.

Veal Steak in Celery Sauce

Makes 4 servings

The celery is slightly salty and watery, a very distinct flavor that goes well with the veal that I spice up with paprika and a hot chili pepper.

½ cup flour
½ teaspoon salt
½ teaspoon paprika
¼ teaspoon hot chili pepper
4 slices veal on the bone
2 tablespoons oil

Sauce:
2 medium onions, minced
6 garlic cloves, chopped
1 ½ cup celery root, thinly minced
3 tomatoes
1 cup dry white wine
½ teaspoon *each* of salt, white pepper, and sugar

Mix the flour with the seasoning and spread on the veal pieces.
In a medium-sized pot, warm up the oil and sauté the veal pieces on both sides, until the veal turns light brown.
Put the veal on a paper towel to absorb the oil

Sauce:
In the oil that remains in the pot, sauté the onion until golden.
Lower the heat, add the garlic and mix for another 2 minutes.
Add ¾ cup celery and continue steaming in a covered pot 3 more minutes.
Soak the tomatoes in hot water for 3 minutes, peel and mash them.
Add the tomatoes to the pot and bring to a boil.
Add the wine, the salt, the pepper, and the sugar.

Gather the vegetables to one corner in the pot. Put in the veal slices. Cover with the vegetables. Cover the pot and cook on a low heat 15 minutes. Add the remaining ¾ cup celery and continue cooking 5 minutes. Serve hot with cooked potatoes.

FISH

Fish Smarts

Eat fish once or twice a week. Fish can significantly reduce the risk of heart attack. The protective value of fish comes from the type of polyunsaturated fatty acids called Omega-3s found in its oil.

Choose tuna, whether you choose white, light, solid, or chunk, packed in water, not vegetable or soybean oil. Even if you drain most of the added oil, you still increase the fat and calorie count by more than 50%.

Chunk light tuna is consistently the lowest in fat.

Red Snapper Baked in Vegetables

Makes 2 servings

2 fresh tomatoes cut into ½-inch slices
1 red pepper, sliced
1 large onion, sliced
2 tablespoons butter
¼ cup white wine
2 garlic cloves, minced
1 teaspoon dried basil
1 teaspoon dried thyme
Salt and black pepper
2 whole red snappers, 1 pound each
½ cup pitted green olives

In a bowl, put the tomatoes, red pepper, and onion.
In a separate bowl, mix the butter with the wine, the garlic, the condiments, and salt and pepper.
In a large ovenproof pan, put ¼ of the tomatoes and onion and pour in half of the condiment mix.
Put the fish into the ovenproof pan. Cover each fish with the rest of the tomato and onion sauce.
Pour in the rest of the condiment mix. Sprinkle the olives on top.
Bake at 450° for 30 minutes.
Serve hot.

FISH

Halibut Baked in Wine

Makes 4 servings

Fish is very delicious and you can use a wide range of delectable fish varieties for all your fish recipes.

- 1 teaspoon oil or margarine
- 4 pieces halibut, 8 ounces each
- 2 shallots, chopped
- 1 tomato, diced
- ½ cup dry white wine
- 1 ½ cups water
- 1 tablespoon dried mint
- 1 tablespoon cornstarch, diluted in a little water
- 1 cup plain yogurt

Preheat oven to 400°. Grease a baking dish with oil or margarine and place the pieces of fish in it.
Add the chopped shallot and the diced tomato on top.
Add the wine and water and sprinkle the mint.
Bake for 15 minutes. Remove the fish from oven and keep in warm place.
Pour the fish stock into a saucepan, heat and add the diluted cornstarch.
Mix thoroughly. Add the yogurt and simmer. Do not bring to boil.
Transfer the fish to a serving plate and pour the sauce on top.
Serve immediately with spaghetti.

Salmon Fillet in Tomato Sauce

Makes 4 servings

Salmon is reborn with this sweet and tangy tomato sauce. If using fresh tomatoes, pick only the ripest. They will give you plenty of juice and sweetness.

4 pieces salmon fillet, 6 ounces each
1 ounce butter
1 tablespoon olive oil
Salt and freshly ground black pepper

Sauce:
1 onion, thinly minced
2 garlic cloves, minced
1 tablespoon olive oil
1 15-ounce can tomato sauce, or 1 pound fresh tomatoes, minced
1 teaspoon fresh lemon juice
1 tablespoon dried oregano
1 tablespoon dried basil
1 teaspoon sugar
½ teaspoon salt
¼ teaspoon black pepper
1 8-ounce container sour cream

Sauté the salmon pieces, 2 minutes each side, in butter and a tablespoon olive oil. Season with salt and pepper. Remove from heat and keep in a warm place.

Sauce:
Sauté the onion and the garlic. Add the tomatoes, the lemon juice, the condiments and the sugar. Bring to a boil for 5 minutes and lower the heat. Add the sour cream until you get a thick sauce.
Put the sauce on serving plates and the salmon pieces on top of the sauce. You can garnish with fresh basil leaves.

Sea Bass Fillet with Fresh Herbs

Makes 4 servings

It is traditional for Israeli families to begin the Friday evening Shabbat meal with fish alongside many other foods. I have kept this custom here at home and this particularly delicious Sea Bass Fillet has become a favorite with my husband. Any type of fish can be used with excellent results. However, if you keep a Kosher home, use non-dairy cream and substitute butter for margarine or oil.

2 tablespoons butter
1 tablespoon minced dill
2 tablespoons minced fresh basil
2 tablespoons minced fresh thyme
Salt and freshly ground black pepper
¼ cup olive oil
4 pieces sea bass fillet, 6 ounces each
1 sliced lemon

In a bowl, mix the butter, seasoning herbs, salt, and pepper.
With this mix, apply the paste all over the fish.
Simmer the oil in a frying pan and sauté the fish 3 minutes on each side.
Transfer the fish to a serving dishes and garnish with slices of lemon.
Serve immediately with linguini.

Sole stuffed with Almonds

Makes 4 servings

An easy, everyday dish that you will be coming back to often. The fish is fried quickly to preserve its fresh, mild texture. Combined with the almonds, the taste of the fish brings forth a supremely delicious match.

⅓ cup fresh lemon juice
2 tablespoons white wine vinegar
1 teaspoon salt
4 whole fish, 1 pound fillets
¼ cup + 2 tablespoons flour
1 teaspoon minced garlic
¼ teaspoon hot chili pepper
2 eggs, beaten
2 tablespoons oil
1 lemon, sliced for garnish

Stuffing:
1 egg, beaten
4 tablespoons almonds, chopped
2 tablespoons parsley, minced
2 tablespoons celery, minced
1 tablespoon mint leaves, minced
2 teaspoons flour
¼ teaspoon each salt, black pepper, and sugar

In large bowl, mix the lemon juice, the vinegar, and ½ teaspoon salt. Soak the filet for 30 minutes.
Mix ¼ cup flour with garlic, then the remaining ½ teaspoon salt and pepper.
In separate bowl, mix together all the stuffing ingredients.
Set aside for 15 minutes for flavor to blend. Put the fish pieces on flat surface.

Put on each piece 1 tablespoon of stuffing and fold.
Dip each piece in the beaten egg and flour (2 tablespoons), and fry each piece 2 minutes each side.
Transfer immediately to a serving plate and garnish with sliced lemon.
Serve with linguini.

Mushroom–Baked Cod

Makes 4 servings

You may also use red snapper or sea bass for this recipe.

2 pounds fresh or frozen cod fillets
½ teaspoon salt
¼ teaspoon black pepper
1 tablespoon oil
½ pound fresh mushroom, sliced
3 tablespoons butter or margarine
½ cup dry white wine
½ cup heavy cream
1 teaspoon cornstarch
¼ cup dried bread crumbs
2 tablespoons chopped parsley for garnish

Wash and dry fish. Sprinkle with salt and pepper.
Grease a baking dish and spread the mushrooms in it.
Lay fillets on top of mushrooms topped with 2 tablespoons butter. Pour in wine.
Bake at 400° for 20 minutes, or until fish flakes easily when probed with a fork.
Drain pan juices into skillet. Boil down until juices are reduced to ½ cup.
Mix heavy cream and cornstarch and stir into the skillet. Boil until thickened. Pour over fish. Mix bread crumbs and remaining 1 tablespoon butter. Pour over fish.
Bake 5 minutes longer until crumbs are browned.
Garnish with parsley before serving.
Serve with potatoes or linguini.

Mackerel Stew

Makes 4 servings

Mackerel can be substituted with sea bass or red snapper.

4 mackerels, 12 ounces each, cut into 2-inch slices
1 leek, green and white parts, sliced
2 green onions, sliced
½ celery root, thinly sliced
4 carrots, peeled and cut into 2-inch pieces
2 tablespoons margarine
1 ½ cups water
1 teaspoon salt
½ teaspoon freshly ground black pepper
2 tablespoons chopped parsley for garnish

Clean and rinse the mackerel. Set aside.
In saucepan, sauté the leeks, green onion, celery, and carrots in margarine until tender-crisp.
Add the fish and water. Stir in salt and pepper.
Bring to boiling over high heat.
Reduce heat to low and simmer slowly 7 minutes, until fish is tender.
Garnish with parsley before serving.
Serve hot with crusty garlic bread.

Salmon Cutlets in Orange Sauce

Makes 6 servings

In a 4 ½ X 8 ½-inch loaf pan:
I was looking for an alternative way to prepare and present fish. I originally tried this dish with whitefish, but the results were too bitter. I decided on salmon, which goes well with the citrus and the presentation in the form of a loaf is different and interesting.

1 pound salmon filet
1 egg and 2 egg whites
Salt and freshly ground black pepper
1 pint heavy cream

Sauce:
1 cup freshly squeezed orange juice
⅓ cup dry white wine
4 ounces butter

Cut the fish into pieces and put into food processor. Process until mixture is smooth.
Add the eggs, salt, and pepper. Transfer to a bowl and add gently the heavy cream. Refrigerate for 45 minutes.
Lubricate the pan a bit, put in the mixture and bake at 325° for 15 to 20 minutes.
Set aside and cover with aluminum foil.

Sauce:
In a small pot, put the orange juice and the wine and bring to a boil. Reduce to a low heat until liquid turns a bit thick and its volume is about ½ cup liquid.
Gradually add the butter and remove from the heat.
Transfer the fish to a serving platter. Cut into 6 portions and pour the sauce on top.
Serve hot.

Fish Cutlets in Tomato Sauce

Makes 8 servings

4 slices sea bass or carp, weighing 4 pounds
1 slice white bread, soaked in a bit of water
¼ cup parsley, minced
4 garlic cloves, minced
2 tablespoons oil
½ teaspoon ginger powder
½ teaspoon cumin
¼ teaspoon turmeric
½ teaspoon salt
¼ teaspoon black pepper

Sauce:
1 large onion, minced
1 pound tomatoes, minced
½ cup parsley, minced
2 tablespoons olive oil
¼ cup water
¼ teaspoon *each*, of paprika, salt, black pepper, and hot chili pepper

In a meat mincer or food processor, grind the fish. Add the bread, the oil and the remaining ingredients.
Continue to grind until you get a thick texture.
Form cutlets 2 inches long and put aside.
In a large pot, put in the oil and sweat the onion.
Add the tomatoes and cook for 10 minutes.
Add the cutlets and the remaining sauce ingredients and cook another 20 minutes. Add a bit of water if needed. Serve hot with spaghetti.

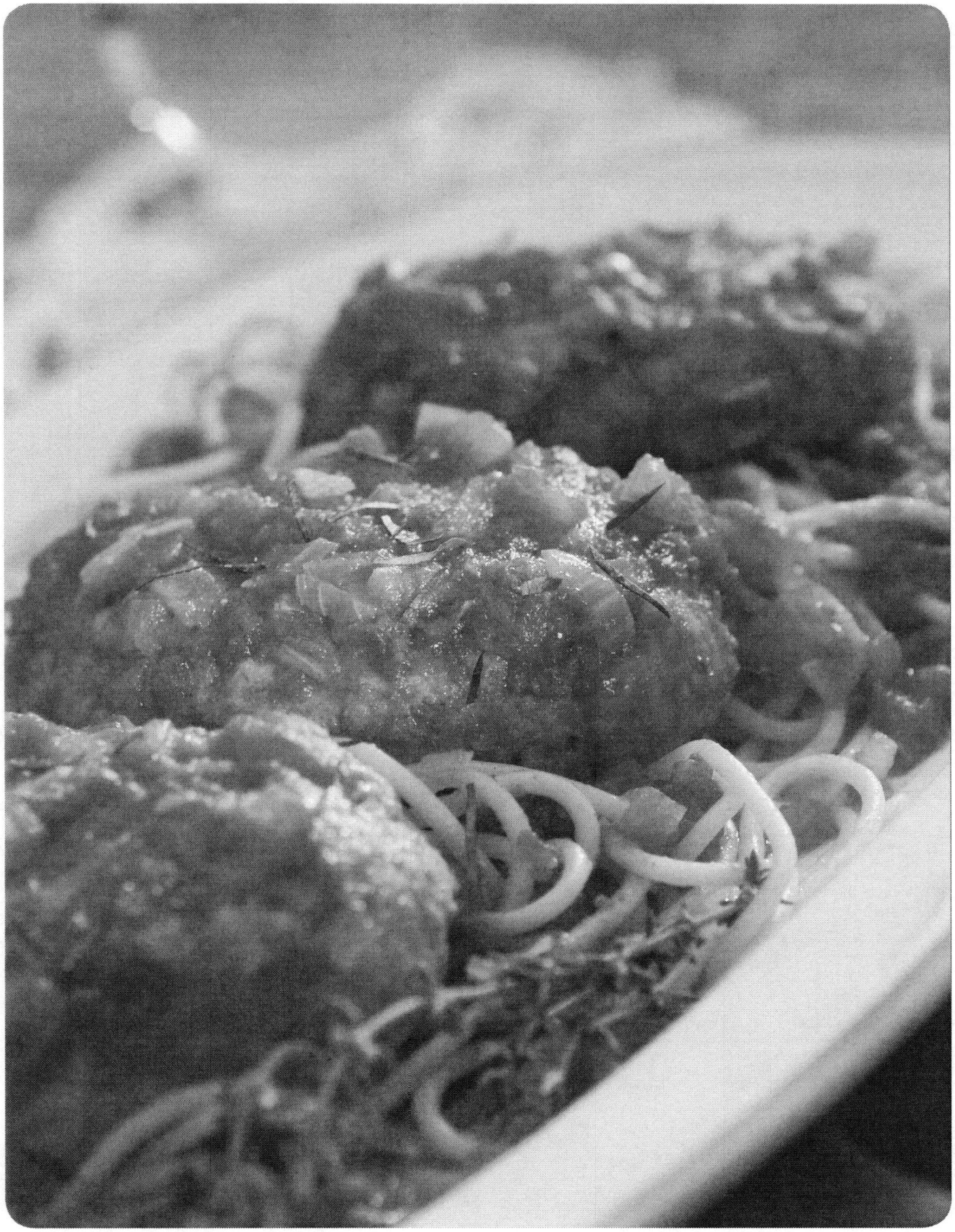

Trout topped with Mushrooms & Cream

Makes 4 servings

You may also use sole or sea bass filet.

4 whole trout, 1 pound each
Salt and pepper
2 ounces butter
6 ounces fresh mushrooms, sliced
2 fresh thyme leaves, minced
¼ cup dry white wine
4 ounces heavy cream

Season the fish with salt and pepper.
Put the fish in a well greased pan and bake at 425° for 25 minutes.
Meanwhile melt the butter in a frying pan, add the mushrooms and the thyme and sauté for 3 minutes.
Add the wine, salt and pepper and cook for 1 minute more.
Remove from heat and gently add the cream. Cover with aluminum foil and set aside.
Transfer the fish to a serving plate and pour the sauce on top.
Serve hot with linguini.

Creamy Grilled Sea Bass

Makes 4 servings

Use fresh sea bass for this dish. Bake the fish first and then coat it in the cream. Continue baking at a high temperature for 10 minutes more to caramelize the cream onto the fish. Light, flaky and sumptuous!

    4 pieces of sea bass fillet, ¾ pound each
    Salt and black pepper
    Fresh lemon juice from 1 lemon
    1 ounce butter
    2 tablespoons minced parsley
    ½ pint heavy cream

Season the fish pieces with salt and pepper.
Place the fish pieces in baking pan greased with oil.
Spread on top the lemon juice and the butter.
Cover with aluminum foil and bake 30 minutes at 400°.
Discard the aluminum foil. Spread the parsley on top.
Pour the cream, covering all the pieces.
Put the baking pan back to the oven and caramelize in a 425° oven for 10 minutes.
Serve immediately with spaghetti.

Salmon Baked in Eggplant Coating

Makes 6 servings

Only in Israel could this dish be inspired! We have all heard of fish in a potato coating; well, here I have matched the salmon with an eggplant covering and you have a grand fish dish that combines explosive texture and flavor while remaining healthy and low fat.

1 eggplant
2 tablespoons olive oil
8 ounces spinach leaves
6 filets fresh salmon, about 6 ounces each
2 tablespoons butter
½ teaspoon salt
¼ teaspoon black pepper
2 fresh rosemary stems, minced
2 fresh thyme stems, minced
Fresh mint leaves for garnish

Pre-heat the oven at 375°. Slice the eggplant lengthwise into 6 thin slices. Spread olive oil on a grill pan. Roast the eggplant slices 2 minutes each side.
Clean and rinse the spinach leaves.
Cook spinach (without water) lightly for 4 minutes in 1 tablespoon of butter. Add salt and keep in warm place.
Pad a baking pan with parchment paper and put the salmon filets in the pan.
Sprinkle olive oil, season with salt and pepper. Cut the rest of the butter into squares. Put a square of butter on each piece of fish.
Put the rosemary and thyme on top of the fish.
Wrap the pan with aluminum foil and bake for 8–10 minutes.

To Serve:
Arrange a bed of spinach leaves on every plate. Wrap up each salmon piece with a slice of eggplant and put on the spinach.
Garnish with fresh mint leaves.
Serve hot with linguini.

Herb-Baked Fish

Makes 4 servings

For this recipe you may use any fish of your choice such as red snapper, bass, white fish, etc.

 4 large onions, finely chopped
 4 cloves garlic, minced
 3 tablespoons fresh parsley, chopped
 1 tablespoon dried tarragon leaves
 2 tablespoons brandy
 ½ cup dry white wine
 ½ cup water
 1 whole fish, 3–4 pounds, cleaned and washed
 1 tablespoon olive oil
 ½ teaspoon salt
 ¼ teaspoon freshly ground black pepper
 1 lemon, thinly sliced
 5 tablespoons margarine
 Green leaves for garnish

In medium-sized bowl, combine onion, garlic, parsley, tarragon, brandy, wine, and water.

Brush fish with oil and sprinkle with salt and pepper.

Place fish in greased large baking pan. Pour onion mixture over the fish. Top with half of sliced lemon and 2 tablespoons margarine. Bake at 400° for 35–40 minutes. The fish is ready when its flakes can be easily probed with a fork.

Transfer fish to serving platter and keep in warm place.

Strain juices from the baking pan into skillet. Heat to boil and stir with a whisk until juices are reduced to ¼ cup.

Whisk in the remaining margarine. Peel off fish skin, leaving head and tail in place. Spoon the sauce over fish.

Garnish with remaining sliced lemon on top. Put green leaves on both sides of fish.

Serve immediately with spaghetti.

Salmon in Champagne Sauce

Makes 6 servings

2 ounces butter
6 pieces of salmon filet, 6 ounces each
Salt and freshly ground black pepper
½ teaspoon sugar
1 cup champagne or sparkling wine
½ pint heavy cream

Melt the butter in a frying pan. Lower the heat and sauté the salmon pieces for about 3 minutes on each side, until golden brown.
Season with salt, pepper, and sugar.
Take out of frying pan and cover with aluminum foil.
Increase the heat; Pour the champagne into the frying pan. Add the cream and continue to cook another 2 minutes.
Put the fish pieces on a serving plate. Pour the sauce on top.
Serve with spaghetti.
*You can serve the remaining sauce separately as a sauce for the spaghetti.

Fish Baked in Salt

Makes 2 servings

A popular dish along the Mediterranean and worldwide. Fish baked in salt is actually very simple to prepare. The salt crust traps in the moisture and herb flavor and results in a juicy, tasty dish.

- 2 ½ pounds meaty fish (such as sea bass, red snapper, etc.)
- 3 fresh tarragon stems or ½ teaspoon dried tarragon
- Salt and pepper
- 2 packs kosher salt, 2 pounds each

Pre-heat the oven to 450°.
Put the tarragon inside the fish and season the fish with salt and pepper inside and outside.
Spread 1 cup of salt on the bottom of a roasting pan.
Put the fish on the salt and cover with the rest of the salt. (It is important to see that the entire fish is covered.) It is possible to have the salt stick better to the fish by gently sprinkling the salt with a little water.
Put into a hot oven for 30 minutes for a 2 ½ pound fish. Every additional ½ pound of fish requires an extra 6 minutes of baking.
Take the pan out of the oven, break the salt peel by gently hitting with a wooden utensil.
Separate the salt layers from the fish, brush away the rest of the salt, and put on a service platter. Serve immediately with linguini.

Fish Salad

Makes 8 servings

This salad doubles as a wonderful main dish or as an appetizer. You can prepare this dish ahead of time; just add greens and you're ready to go.

2 whole sea bass, 1 ¼ pounds each, fillets
2 bay leaves
1 large onion, sliced
1 carrot, sliced
2 tablespoons white wine
1 teaspoon salt
½ teaspoon black pepper

Salad:
2 cucumbers, peeled, pitted, and finely sliced
1 large red onion, finely sliced
2 tablespoons fresh parsley, chopped
3 tablespoons white wine
¼ cup olive oil
1 tablespoon fresh lemon juice
½ teaspoon salt
¼ teaspoon freshly ground black pepper

Put the fish pieces into a pot and cover with water.
Add the bay leaves, the onion, the carrot, the wine, the salt, and pepper.
Bring to a boil and cook on high heat for 15 minutes.
Lower the heat and continue to cook for 15 minutes more.
Take out of pot and let cool.
In a large serving bowl, place all the salad ingredients.
Crumble the fish into small pieces and add to the salad.
Mix gently and chill for 1 hour.
Serve cold or at room temperature with toasted bread.

PIES

Mushroom Pie

Makes 8 servings

Mushrooms and cheese are a terrific combination, rich and satisfying. In a 9 ¼ X 2 ½-inch round spring form pan:

Dough:
1 ½ cups flour
2 ounces butter or margarine
4 ounces sour cream.
¼ teaspoon salt
2 teaspoons baking powder

Filling:
2 ounces butter or margarine
5 large onions, sliced into thin strips
1 pound fresh mushrooms, sliced or 14-ounce can mushrooms, drained and sliced
4 tablespoons milk
4 ounces sour cream
¼ teaspoon nutmeg
Salt and black pepper
3 beaten eggs
8 ounces Swiss cheese, shredded

Dough:
In a bowl, combine the flour, the butter, the sour cream, the salt, and the baking powder. Knead for 1 minute.
Cover and refrigerate for 20 minutes. Grease the pan with oil and pad the bottom and the walls of the pan with all the dough.

Filling:
Melt the butter in a large frying pan. Add the onions and sauté until golden brown.
Add the mushrooms and sauté 2 more minutes. Remove from heat.

Add the milk, the sour cream, the nutmeg, the salt, and the pepper and cook for another 2 minutes. Remove from heat.
Add the eggs and mix well.
Pour the filling into a pan padded with the dough.
Bake for 10 minutes in a 350° oven.
Spread on top the shredded cheese and continue to bake for about 30 minutes until golden brown. Chill a bit before serving.
Serve with green salad.

Leek Pie with Mustard

Makes 4 servings

In an 8-inch square Pyrex

6 fresh leeks, green and white parts
4 ounces butter
1 pint heavy cream
2 thyme stems, leaves only
2 tablespoons mustard
3 tablespoons any kind of yellow cheese, thinly shredded
½ teaspoon salt
¼ teaspoon crushed fresh black pepper

Clean and rinse the leeks well. Chop them up into 6-inch pieces. It comes to 2 pieces from each leek. Cook the leeks in salt water for 10 minutes.
Put the leeks into the Pyrex. Mix the rest of the ingredients and pour on top of the leeks.
Bake in 350° pre-heated oven for 25 minutes.
Serve as a main dish with a green salad.

Onion Pie

Makes 8 servings

In an 11x7-inch baking pan:
A hearty pie with loads of condiments, this dish is truly extraordinary and delicious.

- 4 ounces butter
- 2 pounds onion, cut into small cubes
- 3 eggs
- ½ pint heavy cream
- 4 ounces Swiss cheese
- 4 tablespoons flour
- 2 teaspoons dried marjoram
- 1 teaspoon salt
- ½ teaspoon white pepper
- ½ teaspoon nutmeg
- 1 8-ounce container sour cream

Line the baking pan bottom with parchment paper.
Pre-heat the oven to a 350 °.
Put the butter in a pot and sauté onion lightly.
Remove from heat and cool for 5 minutes.
Add the eggs, heavy cream, cheese, flour and the condiments. Mix well.
Pour the mixture into the pan and bake in pre-heated oven for 30 minutes. Let cool. Cut into squares.
Serve at room temperature with 1 tablespoon sour cream on each square.

Sweet Potato Pie with Pecan Nuts

Makes 8 servings

I discovered this recipe in the United States during the Thanksgiving Holiday and fell in love with it. A tasty, sweet, and nutritious pie that can be prepared in advance. American food at its finest!

In a 7 x 11-inch baking pan:

3 pounds sweet potatoes or yams
4 ounces soft margarine
2 tablespoons brown sugar
2 teaspoons grated lemon peel
2 teaspoons grated orange peel
2 eggs, beaten
¾ cup pecan nuts, coarsely chopped

Pre-heat the oven at 350°. Place the yams or sweet potatoes in a baking pan. Pierce each with a fork. Bake until tender, about an hour and a half. Chill the potatoes, peel, and mash.
Mix in the margarine, the sugar, the lemon peel, and the orange peel.
You can prepare all the above a day in advance

Mix the eggs into the potato mixture.
Place the mixture in a baking pan. Spread the nuts on top and bake for an hour in the 350° pre-heated oven.
Serve very hot.

PIES

Cheese & Potato Pie

An Israeli specialty at Shavous

Makes 6 servings

In a 7 x 11-inch pan:

1 pound potatoes
2 tablespoons oil
2 large onions, sliced
1 pound fresh mushrooms, sliced
1 8-ounce container of sour cream
2 eggs, beaten
3 slices Swiss cheese, shredded
2 tablespoons bread crumbs
½ teaspoon salt
¼ teaspoon black pepper

Pre-heat the oven to 350°.
Peel the potatoes and cook them until softly firm.
Cool and slice to ¼-inch thickness.
Heat the oil in saucepan and sauté the sliced onion until golden.
Grease the pan and arrange the sliced potatoes. Place the mushroom and the onion on top.
In a bowl, mix the sour cream, the eggs, 2 slices shredded cheese, the bread crumbs, and the salt and pepper.
Pour the mixture on top.
Bake for ½ hour, sprinkle the remaining 1 slice shredded cheese, and bake until the cheese browns.
Serve hot or room temperature.

Eggplant & Mushroom Pie

Makes 4 servings

During the holiday of Shavous, it is a tradition to eat cheese and therefore, a vegetarian meal is made in order to keep Kosher. In this dish, I have taken eggplant, a staple food item in Israel, in combination with mushroom and cheese to create this wonderful dish.

In a 7 X 11-inch Pyrex:

2 onions, minced
2 tablespoons oil for frying
½ pound mushrooms, sliced
2 medium-sized eggplants cut into ½-inch squares
3 eggs
1 pound container cottage cheese, 5% milk fat
10 ounces farmer cheese
2 tablespoons olive oil
½ teaspoon salt
¼ teaspoon black pepper

Sauté the onions in oil in a frying pan and add the mushrooms and the eggplants. Sauté for 1 minute.
Remove the frying pan from heat, chill, and add the eggs, the cheeses, the olive oil, the salt, and the pepper.
Pour mixture into a pan and bake at 350° in pre-heated oven for 40 minutes.
Serve hot.

Spaghetti & Cheese Pie

Makes 4 servings

My mother's recipe, the layers of thin spaghetti molded together provide a hearty, luscious, and mouth-filling entrée.

- 1 pound packet spaghetti No. 8
- 1 red pepper, thinly minced
- 2 ounces feta cheese, shredded
- 2 ounces cottage cheese, 2% fat
- 2 green onions, thinly minced
- 2 garlic cloves, minced
- 1 egg, beaten
- ½ teaspoon salt
- ¼ teaspoon freshly ground black pepper
- 2 tablespoons oil
- 4 tablespoons sour cream

Boil the spaghetti in a pot in accordance with the manufacturer's instructions, until the spaghetti is ready. Do not overcook. Strain and put in a bowl.

In a separate bowl, mix the red pepper, the cheeses, the onions, the garlic, the egg, salt, and pepper and add to the strained spaghetti. Mix it all together.

Put 1 tablespoon oil in a 6-inch nonstick pan. Warm it up.

When the oil is hot, put in half of the spaghetti mixture. Sauté on medium heat until the bottom part turns golden brown. Turn and sauté the other side. Transfer to a dish and cover.

Put the remaining 1 tablespoon oil in a pan. Sauté the remaining spaghetti on both sides.

Slice each pie into 2 pieces and garnish with 1 tablespoon of sour cream. Serve with a green salad.

Cheese & Spinach Pie

Makes 8 servings

In a 10-inch round spring form pan:

Dough:
1 ½ cups flour
4 ounces butter or margarine, cut into tiny cubes
½ teaspoon salt
3 tablespoons ice water

Filling:
2 large onions, thinly minced
2 tablespoons oil
½ pound frozen spinach, defrosted and squeezed
2 ounces smoked cheese, cut into julienne strips
8 cherry tomatoes cut in half
3 eggs
1 ½ cups milk
Salt and pepper
¼ teaspoon nutmeg
½ cup shredded Swiss cheese

In a large bowl, mix the flour, the butter cubes, and the salt until you get crumbs.
Add the water and knead quickly until you get dough. Make a ball, flatten it somewhat, put in a plastic bag, and keep in the refrigerator for 1 hour.
With a rolling pin, flatten the dough into a 13-inch round disk. Pad the bottom and the walls of the pan with the dough leaf.
With a fork, prick the bottom in a few places.
Bake for 15 minutes at 375°.

In a frying pan, sauté the onion with 2 tablespoon oil. Remove pan from heat.

Thinly mince the spinach and mix with the onion. Add the smoked cheese, the tomatoes, the eggs, and the milk. Season with salt, pepper, and nutmeg.

Mix and pour on the semi-baked dough.

Bake at 375° for 30 minutes. Take the pan out of the oven; sprinkle on top the shredded cheese. Return the pan to the oven and bake for 8–10 minutes more until the filling becomes a gel and the cheese is caramelized. Cover and let cool for 5 minutes.

Serve hot immediately or refrigerate for 3 hours and serve cold with green salad.

You may double the ingredients; prepare 2 pies and freeze 1 unbaked pie for up to 3 months.

Before baking, defrost the pie overnight in the refrigerator.

Tomatoes & Mozzarella Cheese Pie

Makes 8 servings

A tasty variation, my version of Italian pizza
In a 4-½ X 8 ½-inch loaf pan:

Dough:
1 ¼ cups flour
4 tablespoons olive oil
1 egg yolk
1 package dried yeast
½ tablespoon sugar
¼ cups lukewarm water
½ teaspoon salt

Filling:
2 tablespoons olive oil
2 garlic cloves, chopped
4 tomatoes
2 eggs
2 tablespoons fresh basil, minced
3 tablespoons fresh parsley, minced
¼ teaspoon dried oregano
½ pound mozzarella cheese, sliced
1 egg yolk to spread the dough

In a mixing bowl, process all the ingredients for the dough until you get a thick mix. You can add water if necessary. Cover the dough and leave to rise in a warm place, until the dough is double in size.
With a rolling pin, flatten the dough to a disk 15 X 12 and ½-inch thick. Pad the pan with the dough, so that you leave a wide margin outside the pan walls.

Fillings;
In a frying pan, simmer the olive oil. Add the garlic and sauté until golden brown.
Soak the tomatoes in hot water for 3 minutes. Peel, remove the seeds, and cut into small cubes. Add the tomato cubes to the pan and mix. Remove from heat and cool.
Add the eggs and mix.
Pour the mixture into the dough-padded pan and flatten.
Spread on top the minced basil, parsley and the oregano. On top of them, put the mozzarella cheese slices.
Cover the filling with the dough margins from outside the pan. Push it in.
Scramble the egg yolk with a bit of water and brush on the dough.
Bake in a pre-heated oven at 400° for 20 minutes until golden. Cover and let cool for 5–10 minutes.
Turn over a serving platter and slice.
Serve hot immediately.

Sweet Potato Pie in Orange Juice

Makes 6 servings

Make it on Thanksgiving or anytime. The sweet potato and orange flavor is a standard that is hard to beat.

In 11 x7-inch Pyrex pan or medium-sized ovenproof casserole:

3 sweet potatoes or yams (about 1 ½ pounds)
3 ounces margarine
Zest from one orange
1 ½ cups fresh orange juice
3 tablespoons brown sugar
½ teaspoon salt

Pre-heat the oven to 450°.
Cook the sweet potatoes with their peel in a covered pot until they are half tender.
Rinse in cold water. Peel and cut into ½-inch slices.
Grease a baking pan with a bit of margarine and arrange a layer of sweet potato slices.
Sprinkle a bit of salt, orange zest, and margarine on top.
Continue to arrange the same layers with the potato slices.
Pour the orange juice and spread the sugar on top.
Bake in pre-heated oven 20 to 25 minutes until the pies turn golden brown.
Serve hot.

Meat & Eggplant Pie (Moussaka)

Makes 8 servings

This classic Greek pie is popular in Israel; my mother and my sisters usually would prepare it for every holiday. It is time-consuming, but well worth the effort.

In an 8 X 14-inch baking pan:

4 large eggplants
2 tablespoons flour
Oil for frying
2 large onions, minced
4 garlic cloves, sliced
2 pounds ground beef (you can use turkey)
¾ cup water
1 cup tomato puree
4 tablespoons ketchup
½ teaspoon hot chili pepper
½ teaspoon dried oregano
½ teaspoon salt

Sauce:
1 cup boiling water
1 packet chicken-favored bouillon
4 eggs
3 tablespoons flour
¼ teaspoon black pepper

Slice the eggplant in their peel. Sprinkle salt and put aside for a few hours.
Rinse the eggplants to wash out the salt and dry them immediately.
Lightly soak the eggplant slices in flour and sauté in hot oil until golden.
In a deep pan, heat oil and sauté the onion and the garlic until golden.
Add the ground beef along with ¼ cup of water.
Cook over high heat while constantly stirring, until the meat turns light.

Prick the meat with a fork to avoid lumps.
Remove from the heat and season the meat with a bit of salt.
In a small bowl, mix the tomato puree, ½ cup water, ketchup, hot chili pepper, oregano, and salt.
In a large rectangular pan, put 1/3 of the eggplant slices, spread half of the ground meat, and cover the meat with half of the tomato sauce.
Once again, put on a layer of eggplant, then the rest of the ground meat, and the rest of the tomato sauce.
Lay the rest of the eggplant on top.
Bake at 350° for 50 minutes.

Sauce:
Prepare broth with a cup of boiling water and chicken-flavored bouillon. Cool a bit.
Transfer to the blender, and while mixing, add eggs, one after the other, as well as the flour and the pepper.
Take the pie out of the oven, pour the sauce on top, and bake for another 10 minutes.
Let it cool in the oven for 30 minutes, so that you will be able to slice into portions.
Serve moderately hot.
Pie will keep freshly frozen for up to 3 months.

COOKING
WITH LOVE

Did you ever think there could be "nothing new under the sun?" Ruth Milstein dispels this notion with her new book for American cuisine. Little is known about the wide array of exotic yet comfortable and easy–to–make food associated with the Mediterranean and Israeli cuisine, so Ruth Milstein sheds light on this unknown delight. Exploring this expansive gourmet's heaven with recipes that are eye openers for the experienced chef as well as the novice cook, *Cooking With Love* brings New Israeli Cuisine to The States. *Cooking With Love* offers an amalgam of dishes to meet every connoisseur's desire, including specific sections like Lamb, Lamb Stew with Black Olives; Pies, like Cheese and Spinach Pie; Rice, showing how to make Rice with Green Peas; and Breads, like the American favorite Glazed Banana Bread. So throw out those boring, tired weeknight recipes and make your meals sizzle with these enticing Mediterranean ideas.

Audio Book Of This Title Also Available!

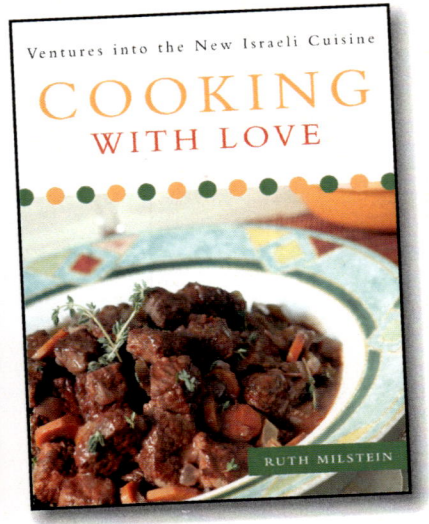

r3mor@aol.com

for more information or to place an order, contact:

TATE PUBLISHING & *Enterprises*

www.tatepublishing.com/bookstore
888.361.9473

Ruth Milstein

Fudge Chocolate Layer Cake
p. 295

Tofu Squares in Ginger
p. 235

Spaghetti in Olive Sauce
p. 195

Chocolate Mousse Cookies
p. 298

Sweet Potato Pie with Pecans
p. 174

Blueberry, Mango, and
Lemon Sauces p. 254, 258, & 257

Artichoke Peas and
Asparagus Salad p. 80

Red Rice with Dried Fruits
p. 214

Radish Apple Salad
p. 84

Mayo-Onion, Sour Cream Tomato, & Taragon Sauces
p. 250, 251, 246

Qince Jam p. 290

Low Calorie Blintzes
with Mushrooms p. 332

Fish Cutlets in Tomato Sauce
p. 158

Rice with Dried Fruit
p. 208

Mushroom Pie
p. 170

Zuccini Bread
p. 220

PASTA

PASTA

Spaghetti in Olive Sauce

Makes 8 servings

A simple, delicious Italian-styled dish. Usually, we add olives to a dish almost as an afterthought or like a garnish. In the Mediterranean, the olive is king and the focus on olives here certainly brings out their royalty.

- 2 garlic cloves, minced
- 8 ounces black pitted olives, minced
    (You can mix black and green olives.)
- 3 tablespoons olive oil
- 1 pound spaghetti No. 8
- 2 tablespoons parsley, minced
- ½ teaspoon salt

Soak the garlic and the olives in half the amount of oil for a few hours or overnight in order for the olives to discharge liquids.
Cook the pasta following the instructions of the manufacturer.
Meanwhile, simmer the rest of the oil in a frying pan; add the olives and the garlic. Add 1 ½ tablespoons parsley and the salt and cook on a low heat for 5 minutes.
Strain the spaghetti and transfer to a serving bowl.
Add the olive mixture and mix well.
Sprinkle with the rest of the parsley and serve immediately.

Pasta with Broccoli & Garlic

Makes 8 servings

1 head of broccoli, separated to flowers
1 pound pasta, spiral
½ cup olive oil
6 garlic cloves, peeled and sliced
1 large onion, minced
Salt and freshly ground black pepper
2 tablespoons lemon juice
3 tablespoons minced parsley

Cook the broccoli flowers in a large pot with boiling salt water for two minutes.
Transfer to a bowl with cold water. Keep for a minute and strain.
Cover the broccoli to keep it warm.
Cook the pasta in the same water that the broccoli was cooked in.
Put the oil in a large frying pan and sweat the garlic and the onion for 2 minutes.
Add the broccoli and sauté for 3 minutes.
Add salt and pepper.
Add the lemon juice and the parsley. Mix and pour on the pasta.
Serve hot.

Linguini with Spinach

Makes 4 servings

2 ½ cups fresh spinach, coarsely chopped
1/3 cup olive oil
1 tablespoon Dijon mustard
3 cloves garlic, peeled
3 tablespoons fresh basil leaves, chopped
1 tablespoon fresh thyme, chopped
⅛ teaspoon black pepper
2 tablespoons butter or margarine
4 tablespoons chopped pecan, toasted
2 ounces Swiss or mozzarella cheese, shredded
½ package (8 ounce) linguini

Soak the spinach in hot water for 2 minutes and drain. Cover and set aside.
In a blender put the oil, mustard, garlic, basil, thyme and pepper and mix for 1 minute. Transfer to a bowl.
Blend in the butter, pecan, spinach, and cheese.
Meanwhile cook the linguini in boiling, salted water until firm but tender.
Transfer linguini to a serving bowl.
Pour sauce and toss.
Serve immediately.

Linguini with Garlic

Makes 4 servings

4 cloves garlic, mashed
1 ½ tablespoon olive oil
2 tablespoons chives, chopped
½ package (8 ounce) linguini
Salt and black pepper
2 slices Swiss cheese, shredded

In a skillet, sauté the garlic in olive oil until golden. Add the chives and saute for 1 minute.
Cook the linguini in boiling, salted water until firm but tender.
Drain and transfer to a serving bowl.
Pour the garlic-oil mixture into the linguini and toss.
Season with salt and pepper.
Sprinkle the cheese on top and serve immediately.

Baked Herbed Noodle

Makes 4 servings

Pasta and its infinite variety of sauces is a great food and the heart and soul of Italian cuisine. I love to cook and eat pasta; however, my favorite preparation is baked pasta. Only then, do I feel that it becomes a real dish. This baked herbed pasta is a savory version of kugel.

In a **9** inch baking dish.

4 ounces egg noodles
1 8-ounce container cottage cheese, 3% fat
1 8-ounce container sour cream
1 clove garlic, minced
¼ teaspoon each dried oregano, basil, and tarragon leaves
½ teaspoon liquid hot pepper sauce
½ teaspoon salt
¼ teaspoon black pepper
2 tablespoons onion, chopped
½ cup green pepper, chopped
3 tablespoons butter or margarine
½ teaspoon paprika

Boil noodles in salted water for 6 minutes until al dente.
Rinse with hot water and drain well. Set aside.
Combine cottage cheese, sour cream, garlic, herbs, hot pepper sauce, salt, and pepper. Mix well.
In skillet, sauté onion and green pepper in the heated butter or margarine for 4 minutes. Stir into cottage cheese mixture. Add noodles and stir until well blended.
Spread into buttered baking dish. Sprinkle with paprika.
Bake at 350° for 35 minutes, or until hot and bubbly.
Serve with broiled fish.

Noodle & Cottage Cheese

Makes 6 servings

This is a meal in itself, yet easy to prepare.

    8 ounces cottage cheese, 2% fat
    4 slices Swiss cheese, shredded
    2 tablespoons fresh chives, chopped
    2 tablespoons olive oil or butter
    Salt and black pepper
    ¾ pound egg noodle
    2 tablespoons fresh parsley, minced

In a medium-sized bowl, mix the cheese, chives and the oil. Season with salt and pepper.

Cook the noodles in salted boiling water until firm. Drain and transfer to a serving bowl.

Add the cheese mixture to the noodles and toss. Sprinkle with parsley on top.

Serve immediately.

Linguini with Tuna

Makes 6 servings

Here is a quick, easy dish you can whip up in an instant. It is good for everyday meals, utilizing simple ingredients and provides good nutrition also.

12 ounces spaghetti No. 8
¼ cup olive oil
4 cloves garlic, minced
½ cup fresh chives, chopped
2 tablespoons fresh parsley, minced
1 6½-ounce can tuna, drained, retaining liquid
Black pepper

Cook the spaghetti in salted boiling water until tenderly firm. Drain, transfer to a serving bowl and cover.
Pour the oil in skillet and sauté the garlic until golden; add chives, parsley, liquid from tuna can, and the pepper; stir over medium heat for 2 minutes.
Add the tuna and mix.
Pour the sauce with the tuna over the spaghetti and serve immediately.

Baked Pasta

Makes 8 servings

In a 7 X 11-inch baking pan:

1 pound pasta penne
½ pint (1 cup) heavy cream
1 14-ounce container mushroom pasta sauce
4 ounces mozzarella cheese, cut into small cubes
4 anchovies in oil, thinly minced
¼ teaspoon black pepper

Cook the pasta in salted water until tender. Do not overcook. Strain and put in a large bowl.
Preheat the oven to 400 °.
Add to the pasta the cream, mushroom sauce, cheese, anchovy and the pepper. Mix well.
Transfer to a baking pan, and bake for 25 minutes.
Cool for 5 minutes and serve hot as an entree with green salad.

PASTA

Pasta with Anchovy Sauce

Makes 6 servings

Anchovies are not everyone's favorite; they are salty and oily. If they are to your liking or you would like to try an interesting combination, make this pasta sauce.

12 ounces pasta
4 tablespoons butter
1 tablespoon olive oil
2 cloves garlic, minced
1 2-ounce can anchovy fillets, drained and chopped
2 tablespoons thyme, minced
2 tablespoons fresh basil, minced
¼ teaspoon black pepper

Cook the pasta in boiling salted water until tender and firm. Drain and transfer to a serving bowl.
In skillet heat the butter and oil, and Sauté the garlic until golden.
Add the chopped anchovy, thyme, basil, and the pepper and cook for 2 minutes.
Pour the sauce over the pasta and serve immediately.

RICE

A Few Words about Rice:

Arguably, there is no easier dish to cook than rice. It takes very little time and effort to prepare and compliments just about every type of food. Most of the recipes in this book call for the use of white rice that you can find in your local supermarket.

Rice should be cooked by means of boiling or steaming with just enough water to cook it through. There are many different types of rice from all parts of the world for just about every kind of cuisine.

For example, brown rice needs more time and water to cook thoroughly. Add one extra half cup of water for every cup of raw brown rice. I personally prefer basmati rice for its nice aromas and great texture and flavor. While it takes a bit longer to cook, it is well worth the wait. If you choose basmati, add an extra quarter cup of water for every cup of raw rice.

Rice has no fat, high in carbohydrates, and I was amazed to find out that 4 ounces of raw rice contains 8 grams of protein!

Rice with Green Peas

Makes 6 servings

2 tablespoons oil
1 tablespoon margarine
1 cup rice
1 cup frozen green peas, thawed
¼ teaspoon sugar
1 packet chicken-flavored bouillon
½ teaspoon salt
¼ teaspoon black pepper
½ cup minced parsley
1 ½ cups water
4 tablespoons sliced almonds, sautéed for garnish

Heat the oil and the margarine in a pot. Sauté the rice.
Add the peas and the rest of the ingredients and mix.
Pour in the water and bring to a boil.
Lower the heat and cook another 5 minutes in a covered pot.
Turn off the heat and leave the pot covered for about 15 minutes.
Transfer to a serving platter. Garnish with almonds.
Serve hot.
*You can replace the peas with fava beans and cook for 10 minutes (instead of 5 minutes), after boiling.

Wild Rice with Vegetables & Mushrooms

Makes 4 servings

⅔ cup wild rice
2 cups boiling water
2 ounces margarine
1 tablespoon green onion, finely chopped
1 tablespoon chives
1 tablespoon minced parsley
2 tablespoons minced green pepper
½ pound fresh mushrooms, sliced
1 teaspoon salt
½ teaspoon freshly ground black pepper
¼ teaspoon nutmeg

Wash wild rice in water 3 separate times. Drain.
Boil water in saucepan, add rice, cook covered at a simmer for 30 minutes until rice has absorbed all the liquid. Remove from heat and set aside.
In skillet, melt the margarine. Add the onion, chives, parsley, and green pepper. Cook over low heat for 3 minutes, stirring.
Add mushrooms and sauté over medium heat for 5 minutes. Stir frequently.
Add vegetable mixture into cooked rice. Add salt, pepper, and nutmeg, blend lightly.
Serve hot with broiled fish.

Rice with Dried Fruits

Makes 8 servings

In Israel, we use rice often as a side dish as well as a main dish mixed with other vegetables. Our family cooks it in many ways. This recipe of rice mixed with dried fruit is usually prepared for special occasions. The touch of extra work and detail pays off in the end; everyone will love it.

- 2 cup rice, basmati or elongated
- 2 tablespoons lemon juice
- 3 ounces pistachios, minced
- 4 ounces almonds, peeled and minced
- 2 ounces dried plums, pitted and sliced
- 2 ounces dried dates, pitted, peeled, and sliced
- 2 ounces dried apricot, sliced
- Grated peel of 2 oranges (orange part only)
- 2 ounces raisins
- ½ teaspoon turmeric
- 2 teaspoons salt
- ½ teaspoon cinnamon
- 4 tablespoons corn oil
- 3 potatoes, peeled and sliced
- 1 tablespoon fresh coriander, minced
- 1 tablespoon fresh parsley, minced

Put the rice in a large bowl. Pour boiling water on top. Mix for a minute. Strain the rice and rinse well in cold water.

Put the rice back in the bowl. Add 6 cups cold water and 1 ½ teaspoons salt. Soak for 5 hours, or leave overnight.

In a large pot, boil 4 cups of water with the lemon juice. Add the rice and cook on a low heat for about 6 minutes. The rice has to be soft, but not soggy. Strain the water and put aside.

In a bowl, mix the pistachios, almonds, plums, dates, apricot, orange peels, raisin, the turmeric and the remaining ½ teaspoon of salt and cinnamon.

Simmer the oil in a wide pot. Arrange all the potatoes in one layer. Spread the coriander and the parsley on the potatoes. Arrange from bottom up in layers, ⅓ of the rice, ½ of the dried fruit mixture, ⅓ of the rice on top, and the other half of the dried fruit mixture and cover with the remaining rice.

Cook on high heat for 3 minutes. Lower the heat and cook in a pot that is well covered for about 30 to 35 minutes.

Turn over onto a large serving platter and serve hot immediately.

Rice in Vegetables

Makes 12 servings

In a 12-cup ring pan:

2 tablespoons canola Oil
1 large onion, minced
½ red pepper, cut into cubes
3 artichoke hearts (fresh or frozen), sliced
1 cup frozen green peas, thawed
1 cup frozen corn, thawed
2 ½ cups rice
½ teaspoon turmeric
4 ½ cups water
½ teaspoon salt
¼ teaspoon black pepper
Margarine, to lubricate the pan

In a large pot, simmer the oil and sauté the onion until lightly brown. Add the pepper, the artichoke, the peas, and the corn and sauté a bit. Add the rice, the rest of the ingredients, and the water. Bring to a boil. Lower the heat and cook for 20 minutes in a covered pot. Turn off the heat and let the pot stand covered for 10 minutes.
Lubricate the pan with a thick layer of margarine and fill it with the rice. Push it in well.
Turn on a serving platter, and serve hot.

Rice Ball Baked in Basil & Seasoning Herbs

Makes 6 servings

I don't think I have ever seen rice presented in the shape of a bowl in itself. My mother would make this dish for festive occasions. On the table, it looks more like a cake than a rice dish. With a mixture of fresh herbs and a most interesting appearance, this dish is splendid and different.

In a 7-inch ovenproof deep bowl:

- 1 cup rice
- 3 cups water
- ⅓ cup olive oil
- ½ cup fresh sage, minced
- ½ cup fresh oregano, minced
- 2 tablespoons fresh thyme leaves
- 2 tablespoons parsley, minced
- ½ cup pine nuts, sautéed in olive oil
- 3 garlic cloves, thinly sliced
- ½ teaspoon salt
- ¼ teaspoon pepper
- 1 bunch fresh basil
- 1 pound fresh mushrooms, sliced
- 6-8 cherry tomatoes

Cook the rice in 3 cups of water for about 10 minutes on a low heat, until the water absorbs the rice. Turn the heat off, and add half of the amount of the olive oil, the sage, the oregano, the thyme, the parsley, the pine nuts, the garlic, the salt, and the pepper. Mix with a fork.
Brush a deep, ovenproof bowl with the oil.
Apply 2 layers of basil to its walls, up to the top.
Pad the bowl with three quarters of the amount of rice and leave a sunken area in the center.

Sauté the mushrooms with the rest of the olive oil until golden brown, and season with salt and pepper.
Fill up the sunken area with the mushrooms and cover with the remaining rice. Layer it to the height of the bowl.
Cover with aluminum foil and bake for 20 minutes in a 400° pre-heated oven.
Take the bowl out of the oven, let cool for 5 minutes, and turn on a serving platter.
Garnish with cherry tomatoes.

Green Rice

Makes 6 servings

1 ½ cups rice, elongated
1 teaspoon salt
1 bunch fresh parsley, leaves only
1 bunch fresh coriander, leaves only
1 bunch fresh dill
2 cups water
4 tablespoons oil
¼ teaspoon turmeric
½ teaspoon dried thyme
1 large potato, peeled and sliced into ¼-inch thick pieces

Wash the rice and soak in cold water with ½ teaspoon salt for 1 hour. Drain.
Place the parsley, the coriander. and the dill into food processor, chop the herbs, *do not* mash them.
In medium-sized pot, boil the 2 cups of water with remaining ½ teaspoon of salt and 2 tablespoons oil. Add the drained rice and cook covered on high heat for 7 minutes.
Drain the rice again and put aside.
Put the rest of the 2 tablespoons of oil into the pot, add the turmeric, the thyme and heat a bit.
Arrange the sliced potatoes on bottom of pot. Then put ⅓ of the rice and ⅓ of the green vegetables accordingly over the potato. Add again 1/3 layer of rice and 1/3 layer of vegetables. Again put the remaining rice and the remaining vegetables on top.
Cover the pot and cook on medium heat ½ hour. Lower the heat and cook for 5 minutes more. Turn the heat off and let set for 10 minutes. To serve, turn the pot over large platter.
Serve immediately with roasted chicken and slices of lemon.

Red Rice

Makes 6 servings

I love to cook this recipe at all the high holidays as well as major family gatherings throughout the year. My mom taught me how to make this red rice dish that she topped with toasted nuts and raisins. Since then, I have always made it this way, as it is easy to prepare and simply delicious tasting! The flavor is truly distinctive and indeed, native to the Israeli people. It will definitely satisfy the most discerning of palates.

- 1 ½ cups nice
- 2 ½ cups chicken broth, or water and 1 tablespoon chicken bouillon
- 2 tablespoons tomato paste
- 2 tablespoons oil
- ½ teaspoon salt
- ¼ teaspoon black pepper
- ⅛ teaspoon hot chili pepper

Wash and soak the rice in cold water for 1 hour. Drain.
In medium-sized pot, boil the chicken broth or the water with the chicken bouillon, add the tomato paste, the oil, the salt, the black pepper, and the chili pepper. Let boil for 1 minute.
Add the rice, let boil for 1 minute; lower the heat to medium-high heat and cook for 15 minutes.
Reduce the heat to low and cook for 10 minutes more. Turn the heat off and let sit, covered, for 10 minutes.
Serve with roasted chicken.

RICE

BREADS & ROLLS

Cheese Bread

Makes 8 servings

In Israel, we buy goat cheese fresh, not packaged. It is creamy and tasty. This bread highlights its fresh flavor. You can substitute a feta for the goat cheese.

In a 9 ¼ X 2 ½- inch round spring form pan:

8 ounces butter
10 ounces goat cheese
2 ½ cups flour
2 teaspoons baking powder
2 tablespoon oil
6 ounces any hard sharp yellow cheese, grated

For baking:
1 egg yolk
Sesame seed or caraway seeds

Mix all the ingredients to a dough ball.
Cover with plastic wrap and chill in the refrigerator at least one hour.
Divide up the dough into six balls and put them side-by-side in a baking pan greased with oil.
Spread egg yolk and sesame or caraway seeds on top.
Bake for ½ an hour in a 400° pre-heated oven.
Don't slice the bread. Instead, tear off little pieces of it.
Following this recipe, you can prepare olive bread or use pieces of dried apricot instead of the cheese.
If you choose to add olive to the bread, coat the olive with a bit of flour before mixing into the dough. This will keep the olive from descending to the bottom of the dough.

Ginger Bread

In a 4 ½ X 8½-inch loaf pan:

3 cups milk
6 ounces butter or margarine
1 8-ounce container sour cream
3 eggs
1 ½ cups sugar
2 cups flour
2 teaspoons baking powder
1½ teaspoon cinnamon
2 teaspoons ground ginger
1 teaspoon cardamom
½ cup ground almonds

Heat the oven at 350° and grease the pan with oil.
Heat the milk and butter in a pot on low heat until the butter melts. Chill somewhat and remove to the mixing bowl.
Mix the sour cream inside, add the eggs and the sugar and whip slowly until the mixture is smooth.
Add the flour, the baking powder, the condiments, and the almonds, while stirring.
Transfer the dough to the pan and bake for about 35 minutes. The bread is ready when wooden skewer inserted in the center comes clean. Chill the bread.
Move the bread away from the pan walls with a knife and transfer to a long serving plate.
Serve with fresh fruit.

Zucchini Bread

Makes 8 servings

In a 4 ½ X 8 ½-inch loaf pan:

3 large eggs
½ cup vegetable oil
½ cup brown sugar
3 tablespoons molasses
2 teaspoon vanilla extract
¾ cup all-purpose flour
½ cup whole wheat flour
½ teaspoon baking powder
½ teaspoon baking soda
1 ½ teaspoons ground cinnamon
1½ cups shredded zucchini, drained
½ cup raisins
¾ cup chopped walnuts
½ teaspoon salt

Pre-heat the oven to 375°.
In a mixing bowl, beat the eggs. oil, sugar, molasses, and vanilla.
In a large separate bowl, combine flours, baking powder, baking soda, and the cinnamon. Combine with the egg mixture. Stir well.
Mix in the zucchini, raisins, (coat them with a bit of flour), walnuts and salt.
Pour into a greased and floured pan and bake for 45 minutes, until wooden skewer inserted in the center tests clean and dry.
Cool the pan on a wire rack 1 hour and turn into a long serving platter. Serve warm.
Zucchini bread will keep for 3 weeks in the refrigerator, and freezes for up to 3 months.
You may wish to multiply the recipe, and bake 2 loafs for 1 hour and 15 minutes, or until a wooden skewer inserted in the center tests clean.

BREAD & ROLLS

Glazed Banana Bread

Makes 8 servings

As a dessert, bread, or snack, banana bread is always a favorite. This glazed version sets the others apart. The following page has a low-calorie version that will surprise you as to how close it comes to the original.

Into a 4½ x 8½ -inch loaf pan:

1 ½ cups mashed ripe banana (about 3 large bananas)
⅓ cup vegetable oil
¼ cup corn syrup
3 small eggs
¾ cup whole wheat flour
¾ cup flour
½ cup sugar
2 teaspoons baking powder
1 teaspoon baking soda
1 teaspoon salt

Glaze:
2 tablespoons fresh lemon juice
2 tablespoons milk
1 ½ cups confectioners' sugar

Pre-eat the oven to 375 °.
In a food processor or blender, mix the banana puree, the oil, the corn syrup, and the eggs.
In a large bowl, mix both flours, sugar, baking powder, baking soda, and salt.
Fold the banana pureed mixture to the flour mixture.
Grease the loaf pan, pour the mixture, and bake in preheated oven for 50 minutes, or until the loaf turns golden and wooded skewer inserted in the center comes clean.
Remove the bread from oven, and let cool for 30 minutes.

Glaze:

In a small saucepan, heat the lemon juice and the milk.

In a medium-sized-mixing bowl, place the confectioners' sugar and heated milk and mix well.

Place the bread on long platter, apply glaze to top and slice.

Serve room temperature.

Bread is suitable as a breakfast.

Low-Calorie Banana Bread

Makes 8 servings

In a 4½ X 8½-inch loaf pan:

¼ cup butter or margarine, softened
½ cup sugar
1 large egg, or 2 egg whites
1 teaspoon vanilla extract
1 ½ cups mashed ripe banana (about 3 large or 4 small bananas)
1 ½ cups flour
½ teaspoon baking soda
2 teaspoons baking powder
1 cup whole bran cereal
½ cup chopped walnuts
½ teaspoon salt

Pre-heat the oven to 350 °.
In a large bowl with electric mixer at high speed, beat butter, sugar, eggs, and vanilla extract. Beat until ingredients are smooth.
Add the mashed banana and stir with a wooden spoon until well mixed.
Add the flour, the baking soda, the baking powder, the bran cereal, the walnuts and the salt. Mix just until smooth.
Grease the pan, and pour the mixture. Bake in preheated oven for 1 hour until bread turns golden and wooden skewer inserted in the center comes clean.
Remove from oven, and let cool on wire rack before serving.
Serve room temperature.
*Bread suitable for breakfast and keeps freshly frozen 2 months. Wrap the bread tightly in aluminum foil, place in plastic bag. and freeze.

Lemon Bread

Makes 8 servings

Quite unusual, yet it's not too lemony and it is really a treat.
In a 4 ½ X 8 ½-inch loaf pan:

¾ cup sugar
3 tablespoons oil
2 tablespoons fresh lemon juice
2 eggs
1 ¾ cups flour
2 ½ teaspoons baking powder
½ teaspoon salt
½ cup milk
1 tablespoon grated lemon rind
Lemon Glaze:
2 tablespoons sugar
1 tablespoon fresh lemon juice

In medium-sized bowl, mix sugar and oil. Stir in lemon juice.
Add eggs one at a time, beating thoroughly after each addition.
In a second bowl, mix flour, baking powder, and salt.
Add flour mixture to the egg mixture.
Add milk and lemon rind. Blend well.
Spread into a greased and lightly floured loaf pan. Bake at 325° for 45 minutes until wooden skewer inserted in the center comes out clean.

Lemon Glaze:
Mix sugar and lemon juice and brush half of mixture to top of the bread.
Return to oven for 5 minutes. Brush again with remaining glaze and bake for another 3 minutes.
Let pan cool on wire rack for 20 minutes.
Turn bread out of pan and cool.
Bread is best next day.

Pumpkin Bread

Makes 8 serving

This recipe can be whipped up in a jiffy!
In a 4½X 8½-inch loaf pan:

1 ¾ cups flour
¾ cup granulated sugar
¾ cup brown sugar
¼ teaspoon baking powder
1 teaspoon baking soda
½ teaspoons salt
½ teaspoon each cinnamon, nutmeg, and clove
½ cup oil
1 cup canned pumpkin
2 eggs

In a big bowl mix flour, sugars, baking powder, baking soda, salt, and spices.
Mix in oil and pumpkin, stirring until well combined.
Add eggs, one at a time, blending thoroughly.
Pour into greased and floured loaf pan.
Bake at 350° for 40 minutes, until wooden skewer inserted in the center comes clean.
Let stand out in pan on wire rack for 15 minutes.
Turn out of pan. Cool.
Pumpkin bread can be nicely frozen for 1 month.
*Make 2 loaves by doubling the ingredients. Bake the 2 loaves for 55 minutes until wooden skewer inserted in the center comes clean.

BREAD & ROLLS

Breakfast Rolls

Makes 30 rolls

⅓ cup lukewarm water to dissolve the yeast
2 tablespoons sugar
2 ounces fresh yeast
7 cups flour
3 eggs (2 for the mix; 1 to brush the rolls)
½ cup olive oil
3 ½ cups lukewarm water
2 teaspoons salt
1 egg yolk
Sesame seeds for garnish

Mix ⅓ cup lukewarm water with sugar. Add the yeast and mix.
In a mixing bowl put in the yeast solution, the flour, and the 2 eggs, and mix at low speed.
While mixing, add the oil, 3 ½ cups lukewarm water, the salt, and continue to knead for about 10 minutes. The dough must be soft and elastic. If necessary, you can add flour or water.
Cover the dough and put aside to let it rise for 2 hours in a warm place.
Knead the dough again at a slow speed; cover and allow it to rise for about an hour until it looks double in size.
*At this point you may freeze the dough or put part of it away for a period of up to 3 months. Then you have to defrost the dough at room temperature before baking.
Tear the dough into 30 to 35 equal pieces and make a round, smooth ball out of each.
Pre-heat the oven at 375°.
Sprinkle flour on the bottom of the baking pan. Arrange the balls in equal distance from each other. Allow them to rise for about 10 minutes.
Scramble the egg yolk with a bit of water and brush the balls.
Spread sesame seeds on top and bake for 12 to 15 minutes until the rolls turn golden brown.

Hamburger Rolls

Makes 12 rolls

1 ½ cups water
2 ounces margarine
1 ounce fresh yeast
1 tablespoon sugar
3 ½ cups flour
1 tablespoon salt

Heat up the water in a pot. Add the margarine and continue warming until it melts.
Remove from the heat and chill.
Crumble the yeast and mix with sugar. After the water solution has cooled off a bit, add the yeast and mix well until it melts.
Pour the solution on the flour, add the salt and mix well.
Knead until you get a smooth, elastic dough. Cover with a wet kitchen towel and leave in a warm place for an hour until the dough rises up.
Turn the oven to 450°.
After the dough has risen, knead again. Divide up the dough in 12 equal pieces.
Turn each piece into a ball.
Flatten each ball with a rolling pin to a ¾- inch thickness.
In a baking pan padded with a bit of flour, arrange the rolls. Stick a fork into every roll in a few places.
Let the rolls rise for about 10 minutes. Bake until they are golden brown, or about 10 minutes.
*You may prepare the rolls a day in advance, up to the rising stage in the baking pan, and refrigerate to slow down the rising process. The next day remove the dough from the refrigerator and let sit until it is room temperature and bake the rolls for about 10 minutes in a pre-heated oven.
*You can fill up the rolls before baking with various types of stuffing, such as mushrooms and cheese, and sautéed onion and potato puree, or seasoned ground beef, etc.

To prepare stuffed rolls, divide up the dough into 20 or 24 balls and flatten them with a rolling pin.

Spread the stuffing on half of the circles and cover with the other half. Press the ends well and let the dough rise for about 30 minutes before baking.

Bake in 425° pre-heated oven for 10–12 minutes until they turn golden brown.

TOFU

Tofu & Vegetable Salad

Makes 8 servings

1 pound firm tofu
1 green pepper, finely chopped
1 red pepper, finely chopped
1 yellow pepper, finely chopped
4 green onions, finely chopped
2 sticks celery, finely chopped
1 large carrot, grated or shredded
¼ teaspoon black pepper
½ cup soy mayonnaise, (see recipe in this cookbook)

Cut the tofu into a ¼-inch cubes.
In a medium-sized bowl, combine the vegetables, the black pepper and gently mix in the tofu.
Stir in the mayonnaise substitute and mix gently.
Cover and refrigerate for 2 hours.
Serve with whole wheat bread as a snack or for lunch.

Cream of Celery Soup with Tofu

Makes 6 servings

Tofu is a protein made from soy beans that reputedly has many health benefits for men and women. This tofu-based soup that takes the place of cream is a nutritious, healthy, tasty choice. I prepare this soup quite often.

- 3 tablespoons canola oil
- 2 medium-sized onions, chopped
- 1 small green pepper, chopped
- 1 head celery, chopped
- 6 cups water
- ½ teaspoon salt
- ¼ teaspoon black pepper
- 1 tablespoon dried chives
- 1 teaspoon dried sage
- 12 ounces medium tofu cut into 1-inch cubes
- 2 tablespoons freshly chopped parsley

In a large saucepan, heat the oil and sauté the onion, the green pepper and the celery for 2 minutes.

Add the water, the salt, the pepper, chives and the sage. Bring to a boil, lower the heat, and simmer for 15 minutes. Remove from heat and let cool for 30 minutes.

Transfer the mixture to a blender. Add the tofu and blend until smooth. Return the mixture to the saucepan and reheat again.

Transfer to a serving bowl and sprinkle with chopped parsley.

Serve with whole wheat bread.

TOFU

Tofu Squares in Ginger

Makes 4 servings

A wonderfully delicious dish that is quite easy to prepare while providing good nutrition as well.

    1 pound firm tofu
    2 eggs
    1 ½ tablespoons oil
    ¼ cup flour
    3 tablespoons toasted sesame
    1/3 cup light soy sauce
    2 tablespoons fresh ginger root, scraped
    4 scallion onions, minced

Cut up the tofu into small cubes. Beat the eggs.
Warm up oil in a frying pan.
Dip the tofu in flour and then in the eggs, and sauté on one side.
Spread the toasted sesame on the tofu, and sauté the second side.
Remove the tofu from the frying pan and transfer to a serving dish.
Mix the soy sauce and the ginger and spread on the tofu.
Spread on top the minced scallion.
Serve hot or cold.

Cream of Lentil Soup with Tofu

Makes 6 servings

This soup is rich, hearty, and filling. It is a truly tasty homemade soup that will please every gourmet in your family. Wonderfully delicious!

- 6 ounces red or brown lentils
- 2 large onion, chopped
- 2 bay leaves
- 2 tablespoons chives, chopped
- 6 cups water
- 10 ounces medium tofu, cut into 1-inch cubes
- ½ teaspoon liquid hot pepper
- ½ teaspoon salt
- ¼ teaspoon freshly ground black pepper
- 2 tablespoons chopped parsley for garnish

Wash and clean the lentils.
In a large saucepan, place the lentils, the onion, the bay leaves, the chives, and the water. Cover and bring to a boil.
Lower the heat and simmer for 20 minutes.
Cool for 20 minutes and discard the bay leaves.
Transfer the mixture to a blender, add the tofu, and blend until smooth.
Return the mixture to the saucepan and reheat again. Add the liquid hot pepper.
Season with salt and pepper.
Transfer to a serving bowl and sprinkle chopped parsley.
Serve with green salad as entree.

Stir Fry Tofu with Mushrooms

Makes 6 servings

The ingredients for this recipe can be easily found at your nearest market, making it simple for you to create an exquisitely delicious meal.

- 3 tablespoons oil
- 1 small onion, minced
- 6 garlic cloves, minced
- 1 pound fresh mushrooms, sliced
- 4 ounces shitake mushrooms, soaked in hot water for two hours, sliced
- Salt and pepper
- 2 tablespoons chives, minced
- 2 ounces sun dried tomatoes preserved in oil, strained and minced
- 1 pound tofu, cut into cubes
- Leaves from 4 fresh thyme stems
- 2 tablespoons pine nuts, lightly toasted

In a wide frying pan, warm up the oil and sauté the onion and the garlic.
Add the mushrooms and sauté until all liquids evaporate.
Season with salt and pepper.
Add the chives, sun dried tomatoes, the tofu, and the thyme, then mix well.
Transfer to a serving platter and garnish with pine nuts.
Serve hot as an entree with green salad and fresh whole wheat bread.

Mayonnaise made from Tofu

Makes 1 cup

Don't laugh. After you taste this mayonnaise substitute, you won't believe it's not the real thing!. I once made it for my husband and he thought it was real mayonnaise. The touch of mustard gives it just the right look. Make it in small batches because it doesn't last long in the refrigerator.

- 1 container 10-12 ounce soft tofu
- 3 tablespoons fresh lemon juice
- 3 tablespoons oil, canola preferred
- 1 teaspoon mustard
- 1 teaspoon salt

Cut the tofu into cubes.
Place them in blender together with all the ingredients.
Blend well until mixture is smooth.
Refrigerate for 2 hours before serving.
Use as a substitute to mayonnaise.
Mayonnaise will keep when refrigerated for up to 4 weeks.

Strawberry Cream

Makes 8 servings

Whip up this dessert in seconds and get a surprising result: smooth, light, nutritious cream that tastes and feels like a mousse.

1 pound fresh strawberries
12 ounces soft tofu, cut into 1-inch cubes
Juice of 1 lemon
2 tablespoons honey
1 tablespoon brown sugar
1 teaspoon vanilla extract
1 teaspoon rum extract
Mint leaves for garnish

Leave 4 strawberries aside, sliced.
Place the rest of the ingredients, except the mint leaves, into a blender and mix until smooth.
Chill for 3 hours.
Pour into dessert dishes, and garnish with the sliced strawberries and mint leaves.

TOFU

Avocado Tofu Dessert

Makes 6 servings

Would you ever believe avocado could taste this marvelous as a dessert? This dish is the perfect answer to your prayers!

6 ounces biscuits, crushed
2 tablespoons margarine, softened
2 medium-sized ripe avocados, peeled and sliced
1 pound medium tofu, cut into 1-inch cubes
4 tablespoons plain soy yogurt
3 tablespoons brown sugar
Juice and rind of 1 lemon
Rind of ½ orange
1 tablespoon minced chives for garnish

In a small bowl, mix the biscuits and the margarine.
Divide the mixture between 6 serving dessert dishes, press down well, and chill for 1 hour.
Place the rest of the ingredients except the chives into a blender and mix until smooth.
Pour the avocado mixture into the chilled dishes and refrigerate for 2 hours.
Garnish with chives and serve as a dessert or snack.

Tofu Apricot Cream

Makes 4 servings

This is a delicious pudding-like dessert. I like to serve it topped with almonds, freeze it like frozen yogurt, or use it as a topping itself on cakes or fresh fruit.

- 6 ounces dried apricots or 12 fresh, pitted
- 8 ounces soft tofu
- 3 teaspoons lemon juice
- 2 tablespoons sugar
- 2 tablespoons honey
- 4 tablespoons soy yogurt
- 2 tablespoons walnuts, finely crushed
- Fresh mint leaves for garnish

Soak the apricots in water for 2 hours.(only if you use dried apricots). Place all ingredients, except the mint leaves in a blender. Cover and mix until smooth.
Let it chill for 2 hours.
Pour into dessert dishes and garnish with mint leaves.

Fruit Tofu Sherbet

Makes 4 servings

4 ounces soft tofu, cut into cubes
4 ounces fresh cherries, pitted
2 ounces strawberry
2 ounces pineapple, fresh or from can
1 cup fresh orange juice
1 banana
Juice from ½ lemon
1 cup water
1½ teaspoons almond extract

Place all the ingredients in blender or food processor. Blend until smooth. Chill for 2 hours.
Pour into 4 tall glasses and serve very cold.

SAUCES

Tarragon Sauce

Makes 1 cup

This sauce has a sharp, spicy robust kick to it. It enhances almost any fish or vegetable dish magnificently while not overpowering it.

3 tablespoons butter or margarine
2 tablespoons flour
1 cup milk
2 tablespoons heavy cream
3 tablespoons fresh tarragon, chopped
3 tablespoons fresh parsley, chopped
Dash of salt and white pepper

Melt the butter in a pan. Add the flour and cook for 2 minutes.
Add the milk and cream, and return the pan to the heat and bring to boil.
Reduce the heat and cook for 4 minutes.
Remove the pan from the heat and add the tarragon, parsley, salt, and pepper. Keep stirring until the sauce is smooth.
Cover and refrigerate for 4 hours.
Before serving, reheat very slowly because of the cream.
The sauce can stay frozen for up to 2 months.

Garlic Lime Sauce

Makes ½ cup

I discovered this sauce while experimenting one day using Asian ingredients. It truly makes a great sauce.

⅓ cup fresh lime juice
1 ½ tablespoons sugar
1 tablespoon warm water
1 teaspoon peanut oil
1½ teaspoon fish sauce
2 garlic cloves, finely chopped
½ teaspoon red pepper flakes
1 teaspoon chopped mint

Combine all ingredients in small bowl.
Chill for 30 minutes to blend flavor.
Serve over raw vegetables.

SAUCES

Sour Cream Curry Sauce

Makes 1 cup sauce

The unique flavor of curry mixed with sour cream can give any fish dish that extra special taste that will please everyone. Try this adventurous sauce.

- 1 cup light sour cream
- 1 tablespoon fresh lemon juice
- 2 garlic cloves, minced
- 2 teaspoon grated onion
- ½ teaspoon curry powder
- ¼ teaspoon salt
- ¼ teaspoon white pepper

Combine all ingredients, stirring until well blended.
Cover and refrigerate to blend flavors for 1 hour.
Serve with broiled fish.

Mayonnaise Onion Sauce

Makes 1 cup

1 cup light mayonnaise
2 tablespoons green onion, thinly sliced
1 teaspoon dried dill
1 tablespoon chives, minced
1 tablespoon fresh lemon juice
½ teaspoon salt
¼ teaspoon black pepper
1 tablespoon parsley, minced

Combine all ingredients, stirring until well blended.
Cover and refrigerate to blend flavors for 2 hours.
Serve with broiled meat or over vegetable salad.

Sour Cream Tomato Sauce

Makes 1 cup

A beautiful pink sauce that I make when entertaining; it goes well on fish or vegetables. Make it thicker and you have a delicious dip as well.

½ cup light sour cream
½ cup light mayonnaise
1 tablespoon tomato paste
¼ teaspoon dried mustard
¼ teaspoon dried cumin
1 tablespoon chives
½ teaspoon salt
¼ teaspoon liquid hot pepper sauce

Combine all ingredients, stirring until well blended.
Cover and refrigerate to blend flavor 1 hour.
Serve with broiled fish or vegetable salad.

Tomato Sauce for Green Salad

Makes 8 servings

Picking fresh tomatoes from our backyard in Israel brings back to memory this simple, yet deliciously satisfying dressing for a tossed green salad.

6–8 tomatoes
2 cloves garlic
1 hot chili pepper, without the seeds
¼ cup oil olive
½ teaspoon salt
¼ teaspoon black pepper
Juice from 1 lemon, (optional)

In food processor or blender, mix all the ingredients until smooth.
Cover and refrigerate to blend flavor for a few hours.
Pour over green salad or chopped lettuce.

Honey & Cumin Sauce

Makes 4 servings

6 tablespoons olive oil
3 tablespoons balsamic vinegar
2 teaspoons honey
¾ teaspoon cumin
¾ teaspoon hot chili pepper

Place all the ingredients in an airtight jar.
Shake well.
Refrigerate to let the flavors blend.
Serve cold over green salad, or room temperature over a hot vegetable platter.

Blueberry Sauce

Makes 2 ¼ cups

The best pancakes we ever had were in the town of Lancaster in Pennsylvania Dutch country. I tried to improvise on the sauce that put those pancakes over the top. Give this a try!

2 cups fresh blueberries
1 teaspoon grated lemon peel
1 teaspoon fresh lemon juice
2 tablespoons honey
2 teaspoons cornstarch
¼ cup water

Place the blueberries, lemon peel and the lemon juice in blender.
Process the berries till chopped, not pureed.
In a small saucepan, combine the blueberry mixture and the honey.
Stir over low heat just before boiling.
Mix the starch and the water and add to the berries.
Cook on low heat for 5 minutes until the sauce thickens.
Serve cold over ice cream.
Serve room temperature with cake or over pancakes.

SAUCES

Peach Sauce

Makes 6 servings

I always keep a few sweet sauces in my refrigerator that I use to top some frozen yogurt, fresh fruit, or a cake that I am serving.

2 ounces butter
1/3 cup brown sugar
1 orange, rind and juice
1 lemon, rind and juice
⅓ cup honey
2 tablespoons brandy
3 tablespoons orange liqueur, such as Grand Marnier
6 fresh peaches, peeled and sliced

In large skillet, melt butter. Add sugar and cook over medium heat, until bubbly.
Add rinds, juices, and honey, cook over medium heat while stirring occasionally for 2 minutes.
Remove skillet from heat. Add brandy, liqueur, and peaches.
Return skillet to medium heat, and cook for 3 minutes or until syrup thickens and coats peaches.
Serve hot or cold over ice cream.
Serve room temperature over sponge cake.

Lemon Sauce

Makes 1 cup

½ cup unsalted butter
1 ½ cups sugar
Rinds and juice of 2 lemons
1 egg yolk

Beat the butter until soft.
Add sugar, lemon rinds and juice. Blend well.
Add egg yolk and continue beating until smooth.
Cover and refrigerate. Serve over pancakes or sponge cake.
Warm up in microwave for few seconds before serving.
Sauce will keep fresh in refrigerator for 5 days.

Mango Sauce

Makes 1 cup

2 mangos, peeled and pitted
2 tablespoons sesame oil
½ teaspoon olive oil
1 tablespoon fresh lemon juice

Place all the ingredients in blender.
Blend and puree until smooth.
Before serving, heat it up for 30 seconds in microwave.
Serve over sautéed liver or chicken.

Orange Sauce

Makes 1 cup

Good over cake or ice cream

    1 teaspoon corn flour
    1 cup freshly squeezed orange juice
    1 teaspoon lemon juice
    ⅓ cup sugar
    Grated peel of ½ orange

Melt the corn flour in ¼ cup orange juice, set aside.
In a medium-sized saucepan, bring the remaining orange juice, the lemon juice, the sugar, and the grated orange peel to a boil on medium heat. Lower the heat.
Add the corn flour mixture while you continue stirring, until the sauce thickens.
If you wish, you can strain the sauce before serving so it comes out completely smooth.
Chill and keep refrigerated.
Serve room temperature over cake and cold over ice cream.

Hot Fudge Sauce

Makes 1 cup

1 cup brown sugar
4 tablespoons light maple syrup
⅓ cup unsalted butter
⅓ cup milk

In heavy saucepan, place all the ingredients and heat gently for 6 minutes.
Do not boil.
Cover and refrigerate overnight.
Serve over ice cream.
Warm up in microwave for few seconds before serving.
Sauce will keep fresh in the refrigerator for 5 days.

DIPS, SPREADS, & DRESSING

Dilled Dip

Makes 1 cup

Fresh dill is a tangy herb from Scandinavia. Here it makes this creamy dip an excellent choice for many hors d'oeuvres.

½ cup whipped cottage cheese
⅓ cup sour cream
1 ½ tablespoons mayonnaise
2 tablespoon fresh dill, minced
1 tablespoon green pepper, finely chopped
2 tablespoons cucumber, finely chopped
½ teaspoon fresh squeezed lemon juice

Mix all ingredients. Cover and refrigerate to blend flavors for 2 hours. Offer with fresh vegetable dippers.

Spinach Dip

Makes 2 ½ cups

What else can be said about this understated, healthy, and delicious green? Just try this unique, tasty dip and superlatives will roll from your tongue. Did you know that the body will not absorb the iron in spinach if it is served with meat?

- 1 10-ounce package frozen, chopped spinach, thawed and drained
- 1 4-ounce can water chestnuts, drained and finely chopped
- ½ cup sour cream
- ½ cup plain yogurt
- ½ cup green onion, green and white parts, finely chopped
- 2 tablespoons chives, minced
- 2 clove garlic, minced
- ½ teaspoon dried tarragon
- ½ teaspoon dried mustard
- ½ teaspoon salt
- ¼ teaspoon black pepper

Mix all ingredients. Cover and refrigerate to blend flavors for a few hours. Serve with crackers or fresh vegetable dippers.

Eggplant Dip

Makes 1½ cups

A great dip that is fun to make and is a healthy alternative to heavy cheese dips.

    1 medium eggplant, about 1 pound
    1 small onion, cut into fourths
    2 cloves garlic
    2 tablespoons lemon juice
    2½ tablespoons olive oil
    1 teaspoon salt
    ½ teaspoon black pepper

Prick eggplant with fork. Bake in 400° oven 30 minutes until tender. Cool.
Pare eggplant. Cut into cubes.
Place all the ingredients into a blender and blend on high speed until smooth.
Chill for 4 hours and serve with fresh vegetable dippers.

Yogurt Dip

Makes 2 cups

Everyone loves the special touch I give to this dip. It is a delicious mixture of cucumber, horseradish, dill, and mustard. A perfect way to elevate hors d'oeuvres to new levels of enjoyment. (You can substitute tofu mayonnaise for mayonnaise. The recipe can be found in this book.)

   1 cup plain yogurt or low-fat sour cream
   ½ cup light mayonnaise
   ½ cup cucumber, finely chopped
   ¼ cup prepared horseradish
   3 tablespoons fresh dill, chopped
   1 ½ teaspoons mustard

In a medium-sized bowl, combine all the ingredients.
Cover and refrigerate so flavors blend for a few hours.
Serve with choice of raw vegetables, such as julienne carrots, sliced celery, broccoli, and cauliflower.

Ginger Dip with Apples & Pears

Makes 3 cups

This dip will go perfectly with a wide variety of fresh fruits.

    8 ounces whipped cream cheese
    1 cup plain yogurt
    ⅓ cup honey
    2 teaspoons fresh ginger root, minced
    1 8-ounce can pineapple, drained and cut into small pieces
    3 tablespoons toasted almonds, finely chopped

Beat cream cheese, yogurt, honey, and ginger root until creamy.
Fold in pineapple.
Cover and refrigerate to blend flavors.
Serve with varianty of sliced apples and pears.
To prevent darkening dip the fruit into mixture of 2 tablespoons of lemon juice and ½ cup of water. Drain just before serving.
Sprinkle dip with almonds.

DIPS, SPREADS, & DRESSINGS

Hot Dip for Raw Vegetables

Makes 8 servings

½ cup butter or margarine
2 tablespoons olive oil
3 cloves garlic, minced
8 anchovy fillets, mashed or 3 tablespoon anchovy paste
½ head broccoli florets, raw
½ head cauliflower florets, raw
2 carrots cut into sticks
1 zucchini, sliced
1 green pepper, cut into strips
1 red pepper, cut into strips
16 cherry tomatoes
½ pound fresh mushrooms
½ head romaine lettuce leaves

Place butter, oil, garlic, and anchovy fillets into heatproof pan. Heat to a bubbling boil.
Serve hot, surround with your fresh vegetables.

Mushroom Spread/Dip

Makes 1 ½ cups

2 tablespoons butter or margarine
1 ½ pounds fresh mushrooms, chopped
1 carrot, chopped
½ cup shallots, chopped
1 clove garlic, minced
¼ teaspoon salt
¼ teaspoon white pepper
2 tablespoons minced parsley for garnish

In a wide frying pan, melt the butter and sauté the mushrooms, the carrot, the shallots, and the garlic.
Stir often, over medium-high heat, until mushrooms are browned and liquid has evaporated, about 10 to 12 minutes.
Transfer mixture to a blender or food processor and blend until pureed.
Season with salt and pepper. Garnish with parsley.
Cover and refrigerate to blend the flavors for 2 hours.
Serve at room temperature with toasted whole wheat bread.
To serve as a dip, add 3 tablespoons water to blender, mix well.
Serve cold with fresh vegetable dippers.

Artichoke Spread

Makes 1 cup

2 artichoke hearts, fresh or frozen
2 ounces feta cheese
2 ounces farmer cheese
2 tablespoons light mayonnaise or tofu mayonnaise
1 teaspoon lemon juice
½ lemon, grated
½ teaspoon hot chili pepper
Dash of black pepper

Place all the ingredients in blender and mix well.
Refrigerate to blend flavors for 2 hours.
Suitable as a spread for sandwiches or as a dip with fresh vegetables and crackers.

Sweet & Sour Onion Spread/Dip

Makes 1cup

1 tablespoon vegetable oil
1 large onion, chopped
½ cup nonfat yogurt
2 teaspoons cider vinegar
½ teaspoon sugar
¼ teaspoon freshly ground black pepper

Heat the oil in a frying pan over medium-high heat.
Sauté the onion for 5 minutes, until they turn golden brown and let it cool.
Transfer onion to blender and blend for 30 seconds.
In a medium size serving bowl mix yogurt, vinegar, sugar and pepper.
Add the onion and mix well.
Cover and refrigerate to blend flavor for a few hours.
Serve room temperature with toasted French bread.
Serve cold as a vegetable dipper.

Tarragon Vinaigrette Dressing

Makes ½ cup

⅓ cup white wine vinegar
1 tablespoon olive oil
2 tablespoons sugar
1½ teaspoons dried tarragon
1 clove garlic, minced
¼ teaspoon fresh ground black pepper

Place all the ingredients in a small bowl. Stir well. Cover and refrigerate to blend flavor for 1 hour. Serve cold over green salad or over vegetables.

Honey Yogurt Dressing

Makes 1 ½ cups

An easy to make, great tasting dressing.

1 cup plain low-fat yogurt
3 tablespoons honey
1 tablespoon brown sugar
1 tablespoon fresh ginger, minced
2 tablespoons grated orange zest
1 ½ tablespoons fresh lemon juice
3 tablespoons poppy seeds

Place all the ingredients except the poppy seeds in a medium-sized bowl.
Stir until smooth.
Stir in the poppy seeds.
Cover and refrigerate for 3 hours to blend flavor.
Serve cold with a selection of fresh fruits.
Serve room temperature over broiled fish.

BEVERAGES, SHERBETS, & COMPOTES

Seasoned Hot Wine

Makes 6 servings

I enjoy iced tea, but one day I added wine to it and served it hot. Much to my surprise, a new and delicious combination was born!

- 4 cups semi-dry white wine
- 1 cup strong tea
- ½ cup sugar
- Juice from ½ lemon
- Juice from ½ orange
- 2 whole cloves
- 1½ teaspoons cinnamon

Place all the ingredients in a large pot.
Cook on low heat, up to the boiling point.
Serve hot with any entrée or as a drink on a cold night.

BEVERAGES, SHERBERTS, & COMPOTES

BEVERAGES, SHERBERTS, & COMPOTES

Watermelon Ice

Makes 4 servings

2 pounds watermelon cut into chunks, rind and seeds removed
2 tablespoons fresh lemon juice
½ lemon, sliced

Place watermelon and lemon juice in a blender and process until chunky smooth.
Freeze for 30 minutes in a small cake pan. Take it out of the freezer and stir well, then freeze again for another 30 minutes.
Serve in a tall chilled glass with lemon slices.

Apple Lemon Sherbet

Makes 6 servings

1 16-ounce jar apple sauce
½ cup frozen apple juice concentrate, thawed
¼ cup fresh lemon juice
1 egg white, (optional)
½ teaspoon cinnamon
1 fresh lemon, sliced

In a blender process apple sauce until smooth.
Add the juice concentrate, lemon juice, and egg white. Process until frothy.
Pour the mixture into an 8-inch square pan; cover and freeze for 2 hours.
Transfer the mixture again to a blender and process until smooth.
Transfer immediately to 6 tall glasses; sprinkle with a bit of cinnamon and slice of fresh lemon.

Soy Honey Sherbet

Makes 2 servings

Basically, this is a cinnamon tea sherbet. The soy powder gives it its richness and thickness, almost like ice cream.

4 teaspoons soy powder
3 teaspoons honey
2 cups strong tea
½ teaspoon cinnamon
½ teaspoon vanilla extract

Mix the soy powder, the honey, and ¼ cup tea. Blend well.
Add the cinnamon, the vanilla extract, and the remaining tea. Stir well. Chill for a few hours.
Pour into 2 tall glasses and serve very cold.

Ginger Pear Sorbet

Makes 4 servings

Ginger and pear are a great combination that seems to bring the best out of both these foods.

2 ripe, large pears cored and chopped
2/3 cup pear nectar
1 tablespoon fresh ginger root, minced
1 cup frozen nonfat vanilla yogurt
Mint leaves for garnish

In a saucepan, simmer pears in nectar and ginger root until tender. Cool. Process in blender with frozen yogurt until chunky smooth.
Pour in a medium-sized cake pan and freeze for an hour.
Take it out of the freezer and stir well; then freeze again for another 1 hour.
Serve in a chilled bowl and garnish with mint leaves.

Plums cooked in Red Wine & Brandy

Makes 12 servings

When combining red wine to the beautiful ripe plums, this dessert comes alive. The vanilla and orange peel added to the wine gives a distinct, lovely touch.

- 1 pound red plums, pitted
- 3 cups dry red wine
- ½ cup sugar
- ½ cup brandy or cognac
- 1 stick vanilla, cut in half lengthwise or 2 teaspoons vanilla extract
- Zest from 1 lemon
- Zest from 1 orange

Place all the ingredients in pot and bring to a boil. Lower heat to medium and cook 30 minutes.
Remove from heat and chill.
Remove the vanilla stick and refrigerate for 3 hours.
Serve the sauce with the plums over vanilla ice cream.

Peach Compote

Makes 6 servings

2 tablespoons water
2 ounces sweet white dessert wine
1/3 cup sugar
Zest of ½ orange
2 tablespoons peach preserves
1 tablespoon grated ginger
12 ounces frozen peaches, thawed and sliced
1 teaspoon vanilla extract

In saucepan, cook the water, wine, sugar, and zest until sugar dissolves. Let it simmer for 3 minutes.
Add peach preserves and ginger and let cool to room temperature.
Place sliced peaches in serving plates; pour mixture over it. Serve with any white cake.
Compote can be serve cold as a dessert.

Banana Milkshake

Makes 2 servings

10 ice cubes
⅔ cup skim milk
1 banana, peeled and sliced
½ teaspoon vanilla extract
2 teaspoons sugar, (optional)

Place the ice cubes and milk in blender and blend for 1 minute until smooth.
Add the banana, vanilla extract, and sugar and blend until foamy.
Pour into a tall chilled glass and serve.
Instead of banana you can use any kind of berries, or chocolate.

JAMS

Plum Jam

3 pounds red or black plums cut in halves and pitted
2 pounds sugar
2 tablespoons cinnamon

Cook the plums with the sugar for an hour until they become translucent.
Store in airtight containers, sprinkle cinnamon on top and refrigerate.
The cinnamon will get absorbed in the jelly.

Grape Jam

2 pound seedless black grapes
2 pounds sugar
1 packet vanilla sugar
Dash of cinnamon

Tear the grapes off the bunch. Rinse and put in a large pot.
Add the sugar, vanilla sugar and the cinnamon. Cook for an hour on a medium heat until the mix thickens.
Store in airtight jars and place at room temperature.
It is advisable not to open the jars for 2 weeks to allow the best possible taste to develop.

Quince Jam

This rare, dry apple jam is a quintessential dish of Israelis. When they are cooked, quinces become soft and taste like a meaty, tart apple. My mother cooked it seasonally and the taste and texture is totally satisfying and delicious.

    2 pounds quinces
    ½ cup water
    2 pounds sugar
    4 teaspoons cinnamon
    1 teaspoon lemon juice

Wash and rub the quinces with sponge. Slice each quince to 6 pieces, scoop the seed and place them in heavy saucepan, add the water, and simmer on low heat for 30 minutes or until the fruit is tender.

Add the sugar, 2 teaspoons cinnamon, and lemon juice and continue to simmer on a low heat for 3 hours until the quinces turn reddish.

Cool for 10 minutes and transfer to airtight containers. Sprinkle the remaining 2 teaspoons of cinnamon on top.

Chill for 24 to 48 hours before serving to allow flavors to blend.

JAMS

Low Calorie Fruit Jam

If you want terrific tasting jam for your toast without added calories, this recipe is well worth trying.

    2 pounds fresh fruits, such as apricots, peaches, plums, etc., pitted
    1 envelope unflavored gelatin
    15 tablets sweet and low, or 10 envelopes sweet and low
    1 teaspoon cinnamon

Wash the fruits and cut into ½-inch cubes.
Place the fruits in large saucepan and cover with 1 cup water. Cook on low heat for 10 minutes.
Continue to cook on medium heat for 15 minutes until the fruit is tender.
Mix the gelatin in ¼ cup of lukewarm water and add to saucepan.
Add the sweet and low and the cinnamon and stir.
Turn off the heat and let cool for 1 hour.
Transfer to airtight containers, let cool and refrigerate.
Jam will stay fresh in the refrigerator up to 4 weeks.

DESSERTS

Chocolate Mousse Cake

Without baking
Makes 8 servings

In a 9 ¼ x 2 ½-inch spring form pan:

1 ½ cups cookie or biscuit crumbs
3 ounces butter at room temperature
2 tablespoons brandy
1 teaspoon margarine or oil spray

Mousse:
8 ounces semisweet chocolate
1 ½ cups (12 ounces) heavy cream
2 tablespoons brandy
2 tablespoons instant coffee, dissolved in ½ cup hot water
2 eggs

Grind the cookies or biscuits in a blender or food processor.
Add the butter and the brandy. Mix well until smooth.
Lubricate the pan with the margarine; flatten the mixture at the bottom and at the edges. Make the bottom layer ¼-inch thick.
In a double boiler, the bottom pot filled with water and the top with the chocolate, melt the chocolate and transfer to the blender. Warm up the heavy cream to its boiling point and add to the blender.
Add the brandy and the coffee and turn on the blender for 30 seconds.
Add the eggs and mix for another 2 to 3 minutes until the mixture turns smooth and thick.
Pour the mousse into the bottom of the pan.
Cover with plastic wrap and transfer to the freezer for 3 hours.
Take out of freezer 15 minutes before serving.

Fudge Chocolate Layer Cake

Makes 12 servings

In 2 10-inch spring form pans:

2 cups flour
1 cup unsweetened cocoa powder
1 teaspoon baking soda
⅛ teaspoon salt
6 ounces butter, softened
½ cup white sugar
1 cup brown sugar
3 eggs
3 teaspoons vanilla extract
1 ½ cups buttermilk

Frosting and Garnish:
6 ounces butter, softened
1 ½ cups confectioners' sugar
6 ounces semisweet chocolate, melted
2 teaspoons vanilla extract
Chocolate shavings for garnish

Preheat oven to 375°.
Line bottoms of two cake pans with waxed paper and grease paper and sides of pans with butter.
In large bowl, mix flour, cocoa, baking soda, and salt.
In another mixing bowl, beat butter and sugars at medium speed until light, then add eggs and vanilla.
At low speed beat flour mixture, add buttermilk. Add butter mixture into flour mixture and blend.
Divide mixture equally between prepared pans.

Bake about 25 minutes, until wooden skewer inserted in center comes out clean. Transfer pans to wire racks, and cool for 30 minutes.
Take pans off the racks and remove the paper from cakes. Turn layers topside up and cool for 2 hours.

Frosting preparation:
At medium speed beat butter and confectioners' sugar; add chocolate and vanilla, beat until smooth.
Place 1 cake layer on a serving plate and spread with frosting.
Top with remaining layer and spread frosting on top and sides of cake.
Let cake stand for 1 hour and sprinkle with chocolate shavings.
Refrigerate 4 hours before serving.

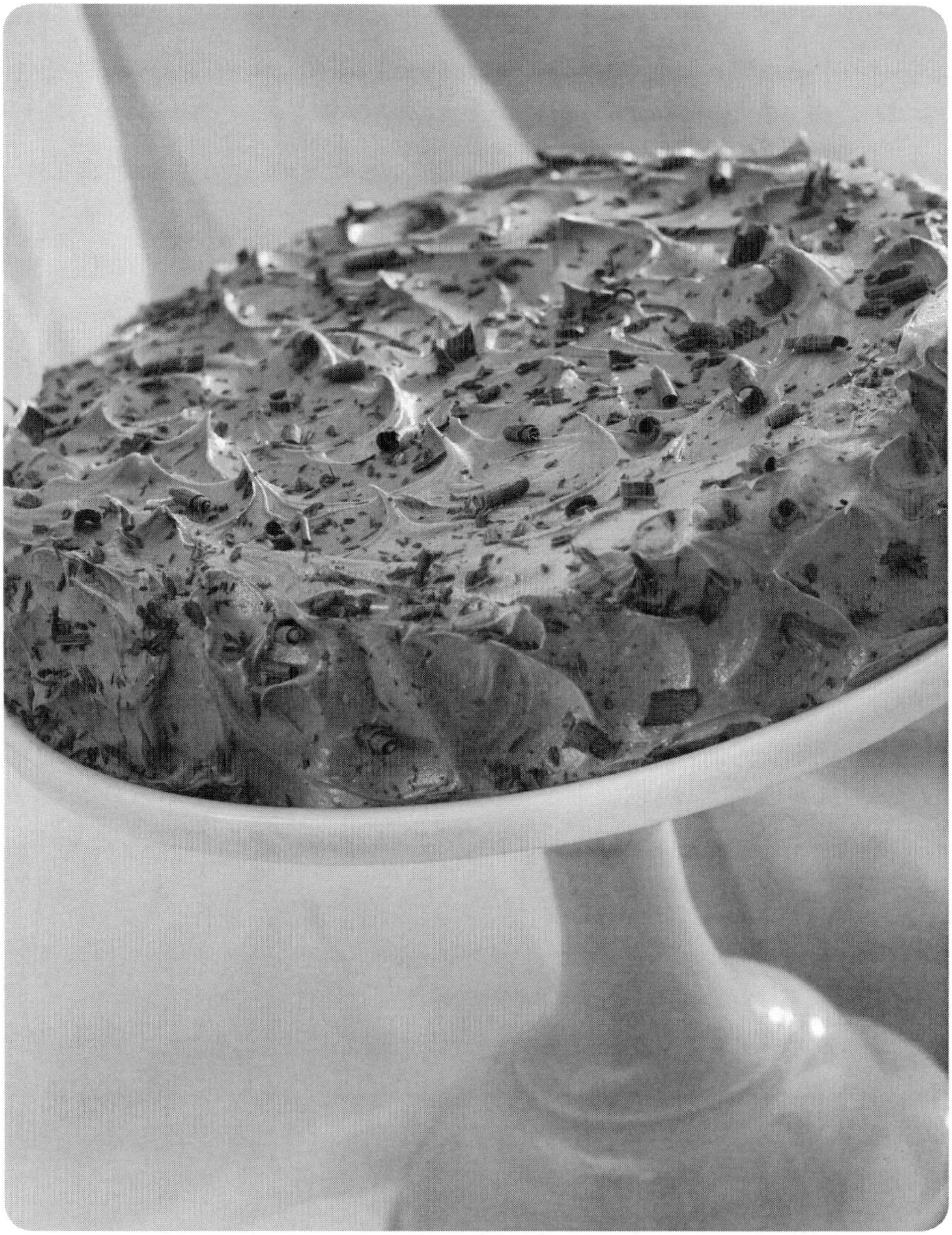

Chocolate Mousse Cookies

Makes 24 Cookies

A delectable cookie made from popular ingredients that I created for friends who love chocolate. This is my quintessential chocolate cookie!

16 ounces milk chocolate
2 ounces butter
2 teaspoons orange liquor
1 teaspoon brandy
Chopped almonds or nuts for garnish
24 small baking paper cups

Melt the chocolate in a double pot: a pot where water is boiling gently and on top a smaller pot with the chocolate. The pot on the top with the chocolate should not touch the water.
Add the butter, the orange liquor and the brandy to the pot. Blend gently and let the mix cool and harden a bit.
Make 24 balls and put on a tray.
Roll the balls in the chopped almonds and refrigerate for 3 hours.
Before serving, transfer the balls into baking paper cups.
You may prepare the cookies with white or dark chocolate.

DESSERTS

Chocolate Cream Pie

Makes 8 servings

A chilled dessert that is dazzling to the senses. Smooth, chocolaty and creamy; all enveloped within a special homemade touch.

In a 9-inch baked pie crust, plain or chocolate:

10 ounces cooking chocolate
1 pint heavy cream
4 tablespoons milk
1 stick vanilla
1 egg yolk

Break the chocolate into squares and grind in food processor until it turns to powder.
Put in a bowl. Pour the heavy cream and the milk into a big pot.
Break the vanilla stick in the length, take out its contents, and put the kernels and the stick into the pot.
Boil the cream and the milk, remove from heat and remove the vanilla stick.
Pour the cream on the chocolate while stirring; add the egg yolk and mix.
Pour the mix into the pie shell. Bake for 5 minutes in 250° pre-heated oven.
Chill for 3 hours.
Serve topped with whipped cream.

Angel Food Cake

In a 4 ½ x 8 ½-inch loaf pan:

½ cup flour
½ cup sugar
2 tablespoons fresh ginger, finely chopped
¼ teaspoon salt
6 large egg whites
2 teaspoons baking powder
¼ cup molasses
2 teaspoons grated orange zest
1 teaspoon grated lemon zest

Preheat oven to 325°.
In small bowl, mix flour, ¼ cup sugar, ginger, and salt. Set aside.
In large bowl at high speed, beat egg white until foamy. Add in baking powder and remaining sugar, 1 tablespoon at a time, until stiff peaks form
Add molasses, orange and lemon zest, then beat on low speed.
Add flour mixture into the egg white; fold in gently.
Transfer to a loaf pan, and bake 35 minutes until golden brown. Cool cake in pan.
Serve with fresh fruit.

Pound Cake with Raisins

Makes 10 servings

In a 7 X 11-inch Pyrex pan:

4 eggs, separated
1 ¼ cups sugar
6 ounces margarine
1 8-ounce container sour cream
2 ½ cups flour
2 teaspoons baking powder
¾ cup raisins
½ cup confectioners' sugar
Parchment paper

In an electric mixer, whip up the egg whites at a high speed and gradually add 1 cup sugar. Whip until stiff.
In a large bowl, mix the egg yolks with the remaining ¼ cup sugar and the margarine until you get a smooth texture. Add the sour cream, the 2 cups flour, and the baking powder and mix well.
In a separate bowl, mix the remaining ½ cup flour with the raisins and combine with the egg and flour mix.
Grease the pan and pad with parchment paper.
Pour the dough into the pan. Bake in a pre-heated oven at 350° for 45 minutes, until a wooden skewer inserted in the center comes out clean.
Cool, transfer to a serving platter and sprinkle with confectioners' sugar. Serve at room temperature.
Instead of the raisins you may use chopped walnuts or any chopped dried fruits
You may serve this cake for breakfast.

Cheese Cake with Mocha Mousse

Makes 8 servings

This dessert has all the nuances and delicacy of the finest pastry shops I've found in my travels. I have improvised on the basic ingredients in order to bring forth a truly magnificent dessert.

In a 9 ¼ X 2 ½–inch round spring form pan:

2 ounces biscuits (about 10 biscuits)
2 tablespoons melted butter

Filling:
2 8-ounce containers cream cheese
1 7½-ounce packet farmer cheese, unsalted
½ cup white sugar
½ cup brown sugar
1 8-ounce container sour cream
3 eggs
8 ounces semi-sweet chocolate, melted
2 teaspoons instant coffee, dissolved in ½ cup water

Coating:
6 ounces semi-sweet chocolate
4 ounces butter
1 teaspoon rum extract

Bottom Layer:
In a food processor, grind the biscuits into crumbs and add the 2 tablespoons melted butter. Pad the bottom of the pan and refrigerate for 30 minutes.

Filling:
Pre-heat the oven to 350°.
In an electric mixer bowl, whip together the two cheeses, the white and the brown sugar, and the sour cream. Add the eggs, the melted chocolate, and the instant coffee. Pour the mix into the pan on the bottom. Bake in the pre-heated oven for 50 minutes. Chill.

Coating:
In a small pot, melt the chocolate and the butter on a low heat. Add the rum extract and mix. Let it cool for 2 minutes and pour the mix on the chilled cheese.
Chill for 4 hours before serving.

Cheese Mousse Cake & Pineapple

Makes 8 servings

A wonderful cake that requires no baking! Just chill and serve.
In a 9 ¼ X 2 ½-inch round spring form pan:

- 1 14-ounce can pineapple
- 3 eggs, separated
- ¾ cup confectioners' sugar
- 3 envelopes unflavored gelatin, ¼ ounce each
- 10 ounces farmer cheese, unsalted
- 10 ounces cream cheese
- 4 tablespoons freshly squeezed lemon juice
- 2 pints heavy cream

Drain the pineapple and keep the juice. Cut the pineapple into ½ inch pieces.

In a double boiler, whip up the 3 egg yolks and ½ cup of the confectioners' sugar until the egg yolks turn thick. Remove from the heat.

Mix the gelatin in half a cup pineapple juice and some boiling water. Add to the egg yolks and mix.

With electric mixer, whip up the cheeses and the lemon juice.

Gradually add the egg yolks and the gelatin mixture. Add the pineapple pieces.

Whip up the 3 egg whites with ¼ cup confectioners' sugar until you get a thick whip. Add into the cheese mix.

Whip up the heavy cream and add to the mix.

Pour into the pan. and chill for 6 hours before serving.

Frosted Orange Cake

Makes 12 servings

A special occasion cake that brings out a lovely, orange flavor; the luscious frosting ads the finishing touch.

In a 9¼ X 2½-inch spring form pan, or 2 loaf pans 4 ½ x 8 ½-inch:

5 eggs, separated
1 ½ cups sugar
½ cup oil
1 teaspoon vanilla extract
1 tablespoon brandy
1 teaspoon orange zest
1 teaspoon lemon zest
2 cups flour
2 teaspoons baking powder
¾ cup freshly squeezed orange juice

Frosting:
1 tablespoon butter
Juice from ½ a lemon
1 cup confectioners' sugar
1 egg white

Beat egg whites until stiff along with one cup of the sugar. In a separate bowl, whip up the egg yolks with the rest of the sugar, oil, vanilla, brandy, orange and the lemon zest.

Gently blend together the egg white mixture with the yolk mixture. Add to the mix the flour, the baking powder, and the orange juice. Make a smooth uniform mixture. Pour the mix into a spring form pan and bake in a pre-heated oven at 350° for 35 minutes until the cake turns golden brown.

If you bake the cake in 2 loaf pans, bake for 25 to 30 minutes, until the cakes turns golden brown, and the wooden skewer inserted in the center comes out clean.

Take out of the oven, chill, and turn over on a serving platter.

Frosting:

Warm up the butter and the lemon juice in a small pot. Add the confectioners' sugar and bring up to the boiling point, remove from heat, and chill.

Scramble the egg white with a fork and add to liquid. Mix well. Pour on the cake. Chill. Slice and serve.

* * * For those who love a "wet" cake* * *

Mix ½ cup orange juice with a tablespoon of Curacao (orange liquor) and pour on the cake after baking, and before frosting.

Bavaria Cream

Makes 9 servings

In a 8 X 8-inch Pyrex pan:

1 ¼ cups milk
4 egg yolks
2 packets unflavored gelatin, ¼ ounce each
1 teaspoon vanilla extract
1 ½ cups heavy cream (¾ pint)
3 ounces sugar
Chocolate syrup for garnish
Crushed walnuts for garnish

Boil the milk. Put the egg yolks in a medium-sized bowl. Pour the boiled milk on the egg yolks while mixing constantly.
Melt the gelatin in a little lukewarm water and add it to the hot milk; add the vanilla extract.
Let this mix cool off.
Whip up the heavy cream and sugar well. Pour the cold milk on the whipped cream and stir gently.
Put into a Pyrex pan and chill for 4 hours.
Before serving, pour chocolate syrup on top and garnish with crushed walnuts.

Orange Cake

Makes 8 servings

Here is the real taste of home cooking. We are proud of our oranges in Israel and this is an old-time favorite our family has been enjoying for years. It is a cake that I am truly proud to say, "My mother taught me how to make." Enjoy!

In a 9 ¼ X 2 ½–inch round spring form pan, or in a 10-inch angel food pan:

- 6 eggs, separated
- 1 ½ cups sugar
- 2 packets vanilla sugar, ⅓ ounce each
- 1 cup freshly squeezed orange juice
- 4 tablespoons sunflower oil
- 2 ½ cups flour
- 3 teaspoons baking powder

Pre-heat the oven at 350° and lubricate baking pan with a bit of oil.
Mix the egg yolks with ½ cup sugar and the vanilla sugar.
Gradually add the orange juice and the oil and mix very well.
Add the flour and the baking powder and mix. Put aside.
Whip up the egg whites. Gradually add the rest of the sugar until the whip is thick.
Gently add the flour mixture to the egg white mixture.
Pour the dough into a pan. Bake for 35 minutes until the cake puffs up and turns golden brown and the wooden skewer inserted into the center tests clean and dry.
Chill; turn the cake on the serving platter.
Serve with scoops of vanilla ice cream.

Frozen Strawberry Cake

Makes 8 servings

In the springtime, I would drive through the suburbs of Israel and stop at the stands to buy large quantities of hand picked strawberries. The superb quality and ripeness of this fruit, truly a "pharmacy of vitamins," enabled me to develop this cool, sweet and healthy ice cream cake that can be enjoyed any time of the year.

In a 9¼ X 2 ½–inch round spring form pan:

1 pound strawberries, rinsed and dried
4 egg whites
½ cup sugar
1 pint heavy cream
1 teaspoon vanilla extract
17-ounce box lady fingers biscuits
Sliced strawberries and mint leaves for garnish

Mash the strawberries into a smooth puree in a food processor or blender.
Whip the egg whites with the sugar to make a full, fluffy whip.
Whip up the heavy cream, add the vanilla extract and gently combine with the strawberries and the egg whites and sugar whip.
Arrange the biscuits vertically around the pan walls.
Pour the puree from the center of the pan and keep in freezer for 6 hours.
Serve frozen, garnish with sliced strawberries and mint leaves.
The biscuits are not mandatory. Freeze the strawberry mixture in a 4½ x 8½-inch loaf pan that is padded with plastic wrap and serve as ice cream.

Apricot, Orange, & Almond Terrine

Makes 8 servings

A delicious cheese dessert that I prepare for the Shavous holiday.
In a 4 ½ X 8 ½-inch loaf pan:

6 oranges
1 14-ounce can apricots
2 envelopes unflavored gelatin, ¼ Ounce each
6 ounces ground almonds
⅓ cup sugar
1 8-ounce container cream cheese
2 packets unsalted farmer cheese, 7½ ounces each
2 tablespoons orange liquor
1 teaspoon vanilla extract

Line the loaf pan with parchment paper, bottom and sides.
Peel the oranges. Cut 2 oranges into cubes and 2 orange into thin round slices.
Strain the apricots and put the liquid aside. Cut the apricot into strips.
Dissolve the gelatin in 3 tablespoons cold water. Add to it ¼ cup boiling water and mix again.
In a food processor, put in the ground almonds, sugar, cheeses, liquor and the vanilla extract. Mix until smooth.
Add the gelatin while the food processor is on; mix for 30 seconds.
Arrange half the orange slices on the bottom of the pan.
Mix the orange cubes and the apricots into the cheese mixture, and put on the oranges. Refrigerate for 3 hours. Turn the pan into the serving platter.
Remove the parchment paper, and garnish with the remaining orange slices.

Honey Cake

Makes 8 servings

Honey cake is a traditional dessert for the Jewish New Year to symbolize the coming of a new and sweet year. It can also be eaten for breakfast with coffee. A low-calorie version follows.

In a 9¼ X 2 ½–inch round spring form pan:

12 ounces honey
6 ounces margarine
1 ¼ cup sugar
3 eggs
3 cups flour
3 teaspoons baking powder
2 tablespoons instant coffee
3 teaspoons ground clove
2 teaspoons cinnamon
¼ teaspoon salt
1 ½ cups coke
½ teaspoon baking soda
¾ cup boiling water
4 ounces peanuts cut in halves

Place the container with the honey in a dish with lukewarm water in order to soften the honey.
In a mixing bowl, mix the margarine and the sugar while adding the eggs one by one.
Mix well until the mix becomes light and airy.
Add the honey and constantly continue mixing.
In a large bowl, mix the flour together with the baking powder, the instant coffee, the clove, the cinnamon, and the salt.
While mixing, add intermittently one time flour mixture and one time coke until finished and when the mix is totally smooth.
Melt the baking soda in boiling water, pour quickly into the mixing bowl, and mix well. The dough should look very diluted.

Pour the dough into a greased baking pan and bake at 350° for about an hour, until the wooden skewer inserted in the center comes clean. Five minutes before you take the cake out of the oven, arrange lines of half peanuts on the top. Honey cake will keep 2 weeks in the refrigerator and freezes for up to 3 months.

Low-Calorie Honey Cake

Makes 8 servings

This is a cake that explodes with gorgeous honey flavor while maintaining a low-fat, low-calorie profile. Believe me, it tastes as deceiving as it looks.

In a 4½ X 8 ½- inch loaf pan:

6 eggs, separated
⅔ cup sugar
4 tablespoons sour cream.
8 ounces honey
1 ½ cups flour
2 teaspoons baking powder
1 teaspoon baking soda
½ teaspoon ground clove
½ teaspoon cinnamon

Whip up the egg whites with the sugar. Mix the egg yolks, the sour cream, the honey, the flour, the baking powder, the baking soda and the spices.

Add little by little the beaten-up egg white to the egg yolks and honey mixture. Combine until you get one smooth mix.

Wrap the inside of the pan, bottom and walls, with parchment paper. Pour the mixture into the pan and bake at 350° for 40 minutes or until the wooden skewer inserted in the center comes out clean.

*** Be careful not to over bake***

Lemon Cake

Here is another example of one of our favorite family recipes. The cake fills the room with the fragrance of fresh lemons and tastes as delicate and savory as it looks. By the way, you can whip it up in a jiffy.

In a 4 ½ X 8 ½-inch loaf pan:

1 cup sugar
Grated peel from 2 lemons
3 eggs
½ pint heavy cream (1 cup)
¼ teaspoon salt
1 ½ cups flour
1 teaspoon baking powder
3 ounces butter at room temperature

Pre-heat the oven at 350° and oil the pan.
In blender, mix the sugar and the lemon peel. Add the eggs and mix until the mix turns light.
Add the heavy cream and the salt. Mix the flour and the baking powder and add to the egg mixture.
Add the butter and mix into the dough.
Pour into the pan and bake in pre-heated oven for 55 minutes until wooden skewer inserted in the center comes out clean.
Chill, turn over a long serving platter, and serve with vanilla ice cream scoops.

Apple Strudel in Fillo Sheets Dough

Makes 12 servings

Frozen fillo dough must be thawed out in the refrigerator overnight, and then defrosted at room temperature for 30 minutes. Then unfold the dough smoothly on a flat working surface and cover with a damp kitchen towel. This makes it easier to work with.

  3 pounds granny smith apples
  Juice from ½ lemon
  4 ounces butter
  1 ½ cups sugar
  1 teaspoon vanilla extract
  2 teaspoons cinnamon
  10 sheets fillo dough
  4 ounces raisins, soaked in rum or cognac for an hour
  4 ounces sliced almonds
  1 egg for brushing
  Confectioners' sugar

Peel the apples and slice thinly.
Put the sliced apples in a medium-sized pot. Add lemon juice, 2 ounces butter and sugar; then cook on a medium heat until the apples turn tender and become dry. Chill. Add the vanilla extract and the cinnamon and blend.
In a small pot, dissolve the rest of the butter. Take one sheet of dough and brush it with a bit of butter.
Put on top another sheet and brush with butter. Repeat this with additional three sheets. You have 5 sheets altogether.
Spread half of the chilled stuffing on the entire sheet surface, leave 1 inch margin.

Strain the raisins well and spread half of them and half of the almonds on top. Fold into a roll shape.

Put on a greased baking pan and spread with egg yolk mix with a bit of water.

Make another roll the same way. Bake in a 400° pre-heated oven until the rolls turn golden brown, about 15 minutes.

Chill and sprinkle with confectioners' sugar.

Serve at room temperate with vanilla ice cream.

Apple Tart in Sour Cream

Makes 8 servings

In a 10-inch round pie pan:

Dough:
1 ½ cups flour
4 ounces butter
2 tablespoons sugar
3 tablespoons cold water

Filling:
4 granny smith apples, thinly sliced
4 tablespoons sugar
1 8-ounce container sour cream
3 eggs
2 tablespoons flour
1 teaspoon vanilla extract
1 teaspoon grated lemon peel
1 tablespoon cinnamon

Pre-heat the oven at 350°. Spread some flour on the pan walls.
In a mixing bowl, place the flour, the butter, and the sugar. Mix well. Add the water and knead until you get a smooth dough.
Knead the dough into a 12 inch diameter. Spread it on the pie pan. Clasp the dough to the bottom and walls of the pan.
Lightly stick a fork into the dough. Bake 7 minutes until the dough turns golden brown.
Arrange the apple slices on the bottom of the dough. Sprinkle 2 tablespoons sugar on the apples. Mix the sour cream, the eggs, and the 2 tablespoons of flour. Add the vanilla extract and the grated lemon peel. Pour it on the apple slices.

Sprinkle on top the remaining 2 tablespoons of sugar.
Bake for 40 minutes until the filling turns golden brown.
Sprinkle the cinnamon on top.
Serve hot or cold.

ENTERTAINING

Fruit Salad with Ginger & Mint

Makes 8 servings

Special aids: Melon baller

1 cup melon balls
1 cup watermelon balls
1 cup seedless green grapes
1 cup seedless black or red grapes
1 cup seedless cherries
1 14-ounce can litchi, include liquid
1 inch fresh ginger, finely chopped
2 tablespoons finely chopped fresh mint
¼ cup orange liqueur

In large bowl, combine all ingredients, mix gently.
Cover and refrigerate to blend flavors for 3 hours.
Serve with vanilla ice cream.

Vegetarian Liver Pate From Mushrooms

Makes 8 servings

A mock-liver pate that will amaze you and your guests! The fresh mushrooms create a wonderful texture and flavor, resembling the finest liver pate you've ever tasted. Your guests will never believe that this dish was made from mushrooms. Liver is very high in cholesterol, so I love to make this mushroom pate that is very healthy. I also make an eggplant and a zucchini version of this pate in the recipes that follow.

In a 4½ x 8½-inch loaf pan:

2 ¼ pounds (exactly) onion, thinly sliced
6 tablespoons canola oil
1 pound fresh mushrooms
3 tablespoons olive oil
6 hard-boiled eggs
2 teaspoons salt
1 teaspoon freshly ground black pepper
1 teaspoon ground caraway seeds
⅔ cup water

In large frying pan, sauté the onion in oil until nicely browned.
Place all of the fried onion with its oil in the blender.
Using your hands, gently tear up the mushrooms into 1-inch pieces and sauté in olive oil until their edges turn deep golden. (The fried mushroom gives the flavor of liver.) Then put them in the blender.
Add the hard-boiled eggs, the salt, the pepper, the caraway and the water and blend until you get a smooth paste.
Remove to a long Pyrex pan, cover with plastic wrap, and chill to blend flavor overnight, or at least 6 hours.
Serve with crackers.

Vegetarian Liver made from Eggplant

Makes 8 servings

Into a 4 ½ x 8 ½-inch loaf pan:

3 large eggplants
Salt
Canola oil for frying
3 large onions
5 hard-boiled eggs
Pepper

Slice the eggplants into ½-inch slices with the peel.
Sprinkle with salt and put aside for one hour.
Wash the eggplant slices and dry them with a paper towel.
Fry the eggplant slices on both sides until they turn brownish.
Put them aside on paper towel.
Slice the onions and sauté until they turn brownish.
Place the eggplants, the onions, and the eggs in blender and puree until the mixture is smooth. Season with salt and pepper.
Wrap the loaf pan with plastic wrap. Put in the mixture and cover.
Refrigerate to blend flavor overnight or at least 6 hours.
Serve cold with crackers or toasted bread.
You may substitute 2 or 3 whole egg with 2 egg whites for each whole egg.

Vegetarian Liver made from Zucchini

Makes 8 servings

Low in calories!
Into 4 ½ x 8 ½-inch loaf pan:
1 ½ tablespoons canola oil
2 medium-sized onions, minced
1 ½ pounds zucchini, thinly sliced
2 hard-boiled eggs
1 green onion, minced
2 tablespoons light mayonnaise
¼ teaspoon cumin
½ teaspoon salt
¼ teaspoon black pepper

Put the oil in a frying pan and sauté the onion; add the zucchini and steam until all the liquid is evaporated.
Place the mixture into a blender.and add the eggs, the green onion, the mayonnaise, and the condiments. Puree until mixture is smooth.
Wrap the pan loaf with plastic wrap. Pour the mixture and cover.
Refrigerate to blend flavor overnight or at least 6 hours.
Serve cold with crackers or whole wheat toasted bread.

Colorful Pepper Basket

Makes 6 servings

The colors of this salad when it sits on the table will almost keep you from wanting to serve it. However, its rewarding taste will make you glad you did.

1 red pepper
1 green pepper
1 yellow pepper
1 orange pepper
1 medium red onion
1 green or red hot pepper

Sauce:
⅓ cup tomato juice
1 clove garlic, crushed
Juice of ½ lemon
5 drops Tabasco
¼ teaspoon salt
Dash of white pepper

Cut peppers, red onion, and hot pepper into very small cubes.
Combine all sauce ingredients and mix with peppers.
Cover and refrigerate to blend flavors 3 hours.

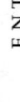

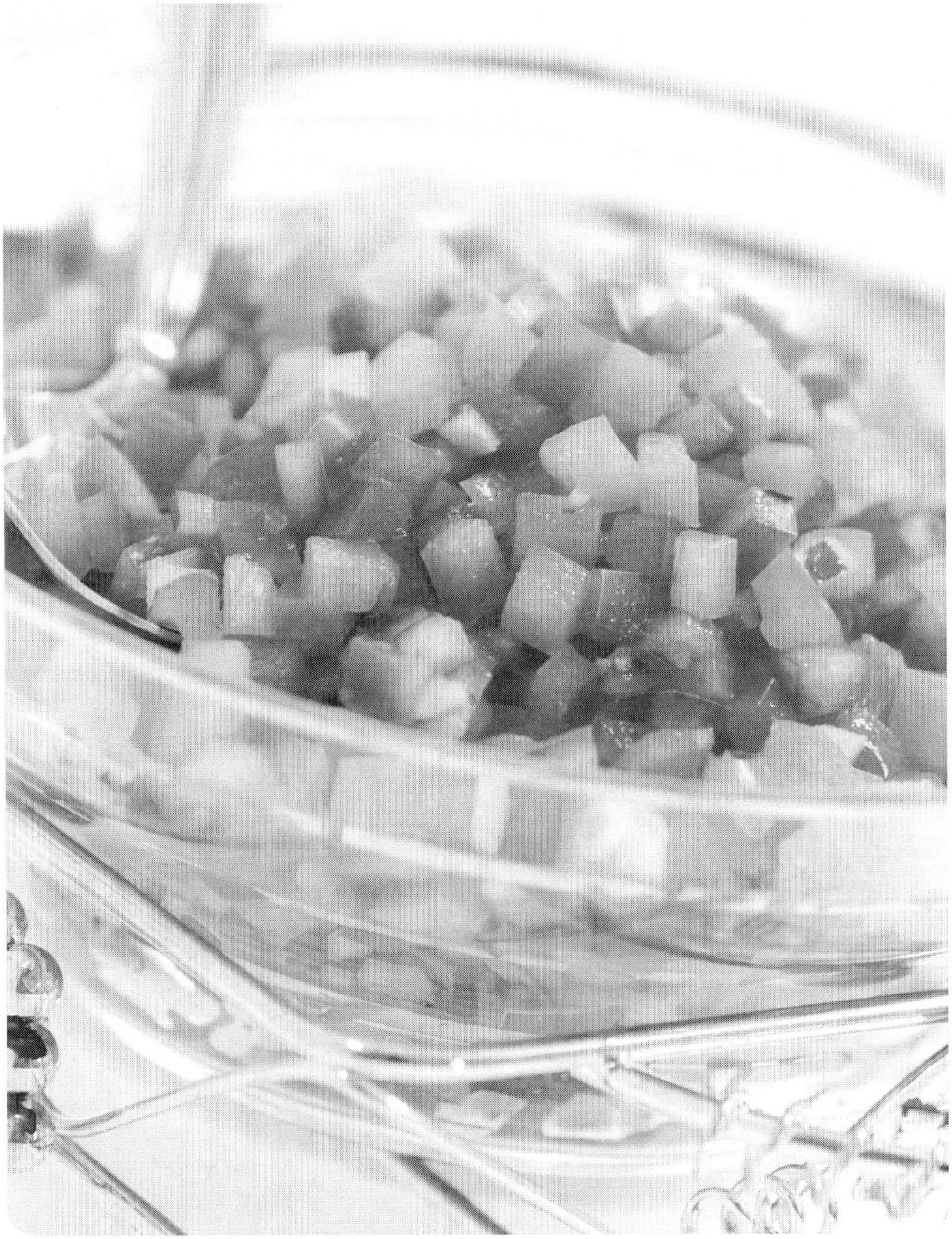

Chicken Salad with Cashew Nuts & Dates

Makes 8 servings

One of my mother's specialties, it splendidly combines cashews and dates to perfectly create a chicken salad that is a gourmet's delight. You will find the luscious dates in this salad a super treat.

    6 tablespoons dry white wine
    2 tablespoons ginger root, minced
    4 tablespoons sugar
    ¼ cup oil + 6 tablespoons + 2 tablespoons
    2 pounds cooked chicken breast, cut in ½-inch squares
    2 garlic cloves, chopped
    2 tablespoons honey
    ⅔ cup cashew nuts, toasted and chopped
    Salt, pepper
    ⅔ cup moist dates cut into strips
    Cherries for garnish

In a big bowl, mix the wine, the ginger, sugar, and the 6 tablespoons of oil. Soak the chicken squares for 30 minutes. Sauté the chicken squares in ¼ cup oil until they turn white. Transfer to a separate bowl.
Sauté the chopped garlic in the 2 tablespoons of oil. Add the honey and the nuts. Mix and sauté for about a half a minute.
Pour the garlic and the nut mixture into the chicken.
Add salt and pepper. Add the dates and mix well. Then chill.
Garnish with cherries and serve very cold.

Rice Celery Ring

Makes 8 servings

This dish might take some time, but the results are outstanding!

2 cups cooked rice
2 cups celery, finely minced
½ cup parsley, minced
1 cup pecans, minced
½ cup onion, minced
½ cup green pepper, minced
3 eggs, beaten
3 ounces (6 tablespoons) margarine
2 tablespoons olive oil
1 ½ cups water
2 teaspoons salt
½ teaspoon black pepper
¼ teaspoon ground nutmeg
Hot cooked vegetables to fill center of ring (optional)

In large bowl, combine rice, celery, 3 tablespoons parsley, pecans, onion, and green pepper.
Stir in eggs and melted margarine until well blended.
Add oil, water, salt, pepper, and nutmeg, mixing thoroughly.
Pour into well-greased 2-½ quart ring mold.
Place the ring mold into a pan. Fill the pan to a depth of 2 inches of boiling water.
Bake at 350° for 1 hour 20 minutes until wooden skewer inserted in the center tests clean.
Let stand in hot water 15 minutes.
Turn into serving platter.
Fill center with hot cooked vegetables and sprinkle with remaining parsley.

Orange Onion Salad

Makes 8 servings

If you entertain a lot, this great salad can be prepared ahead of time. It will expand the limits of your palate with its sensational flavor combinations.

1 ¼ cups fresh or frozen cranberries
⅓ cup sugar
4 medium-sized oranges
1 teaspoon grated orange peel
2 tablespoons red wine vinegar
2 heads of mixed greens, such as lettuce, chicory or escarole
⅓ cup red onion rings, thinly sliced
2 tablespoons vegetable oil
Salt and pepper

In a 2-quart pan, stir the cranberries and sugar.
Cover and cook over low heat, stirring occasionally until cranberries begin to burst. Let cool.
Ream 1 of the oranges to make 3 tablespoons juice.
Mix orange peel, orange juice, and vinegar.
Gently stir into cranberry mixture.
*At this point you may refrigerate for 2 days.
Remove peel and white membrane from remaining oranges. Thinly slice crosswise.
In a large serving salad bowl, combine greens, orange slices, the onion and the oil.
Pour cranberry dressing over salad, season with salt and pepper.
Toss well and serve immediately.

Cheese-Topped Vegetables

Makes 6 servings

2 10-ounce packages frozen mixed vegetables
1 10-ounce package frozen broccoli
½ teaspoon salt
¼ teaspoon freshly ground black pepper
8 sliced pieces Monterey jack cheese

Cook vegetables in salted water 2 minutes. Drain.
Place vegetables in lightly greased shallow baking dish.
Sprinkle with freshly ground pepper.
Arrange cheese slices on top of vegetables.
Bake at 350° until cheese is melted and lightly browned.
Serve immediately.
Can be prepared a day ahead and baked before serving.

Low-Calorie Blintzes with Mushrooms

Makes 12 blintzes - 6 servings

On the Jewish Holiday of Shavous (Giving of Torah), we eat many cheese dishes. The thinly wrapped sweet dough is stuffed with a low-fat cheese, and then topped with a sauce. The blintzes betray its low-fat content with an exceptionally delicious taste. You can make many and freeze the balance for a later time.

2 eggs
1 cup flour
1 ½ cups milk
2 tablespoons oil
½ teaspoon salt
1 ounce margarine or oil spray

Stuffing:
8 ounces fresh mushrooms
4 ounces Swiss cheese, shredded
1 teaspoon oil

Blintzes:
Mix all ingredients, except the margarine. Combine well. Grease a Teflon non-stick frying pan with a bit of margarine or spray oil and warm up. Spread a thin layer of the mix (about 3 tablespoons) into the pan. Cook until the blintz turns golden brown (for about 30 seconds). Turn over and cook lightly. Continue to cook the remaining blintzes the same way.
At this stage you may freeze the blintzes up to 2 weeks and prepare the stuffing at a later time.

Stuffing:
Slice the mushrooms and sauté lightly in a bit of oil. Arrange 2 blintzes in an ovenproof pan. Put mushrooms on the blintzes and spread the Swiss cheese on top. Put into preheated oven at 450°. Bake on top rack until the cheese caramelizes. Bake the remaining blintzes the same way.

This dish is suitable for entertaining, along
with wine, or as an entree along with a salad.

Low-Calorie Fruit & Cheese Blintzes in Orange Sauce

Makes 12 blintzes

2 eggs
1 cup flour
1 ½ cups milk
2 tablespoons oil
½ teaspoon salt
1 ounce margarine or oil spray
Stuffing and Sauce:
6 ounces preserved fruits (strawberry, mango, peaches, or apricots)
4 ounces cream cheese
12 ounces, 1 ½ packets unsalted farmer cheese
6 teaspoons sugar
1 cup fresh squeezed orange juice
3 tablespoons corn flour dissolved in a bit of water

In a medium-sized bowl, mix all the blintzes ingredients excpet the margarine.
Lubricate a Teflon, non-stick frying pan with a bit of margarine or oil spray and warm up. Spread a thin layer of the mix (about 3 tablespoons) into the pan. Sauté until the blintz turns golden brown (for about 30 seconds). Turn over and sauté lightly.
Continue to cook the remaining blintzes the same way.
* At this stage you may freeze the blintzes up to 2 weeks and prepare the stuffing at a later time.

Stuffing:
Cut the fruit into small cubes; mix the fruit, the 2 cheeses, and 2 tablespoons of sugar.
Spread 2 full tablespoons stuffing at the center of each blintz and roll the blintz. Lubricate a baking pan with margarine. Arrange the stuffed blintzes side by side.

Sauce:

In a small pot, boil the orange juice with the remaining 4 tablespoons of sugar.

Add the dissolved corn flour and stir until the sauce turns thick and halfway translucent.

Pour the sauce on the blintzes and warm up in the oven for few minutes or in a microwave with a microwave-proof plate.

Smoked Fish Spread

Makes 1 cup, about 8 servings

Use smoked whitefish, salmon, herring or any other fish you desire.

1 cup smoked fish, bones and skin removed
4 ounces butter
3 ounces cream cheese with chives
½ teaspoon salt
4 drops liquid hot pepper
Chopped parsley for garnish

Put fish into a blender. Process until fish is pureed.
In medium-sized bowl, with wooden spoon blend fish, butter, cream cheese, salt, and liquid hot pepper until smooth and well mixed.
Cover and chill for 3 hours.
Turn into serving dish. Top with parsley.
Serve with fresh vegetables, crackers, or hot French bread.

Potato Salad Baked in Yogurt

Makes 8 servings

Here's another dish that can be baked ahead of time. Prepare the sauce as the guests arrive. The yogurt cuts the fat but leaves nothing to be desired in taste.

In an 8 ½ X 8 ½-inch Pyrex pan:

4 large potatoes, rinsed and sliced in their peel
¼ cup water
¼ cup olive oil
½ teaspoon salt
¼ teaspoon white pepper
2 ounces pine nuts, toasted

Sauce:
2 8-ounce container plain yogurt, 3% fat
1 cup fresh basil, minced
2 garlic cloves, chopped
3 tablespoons olive oil
Salt and pepper

Pre-heat oven to 350°.
Put the sliced potatoes in a pan. Pour in the water and the oil.
Season with salt and pepper.
Bake 35 to 40 minutes.
Puree all of the sauce ingredients in the blender. Pour the sauce on the potatoes and bake in a 350° pre-heated oven for 12 minutes. Take out of oven. Spread toasted pine nuts on top and serve immediately.
To serve cold, or at room temperature, chill the baked potatoes and transfer to a serving bowl; pour the sauce on top, then spread the toasted pine nuts over the potatoes and serve.

Cooked Mushroom & Avocado Salad

Makes 8 servings

A delectable dish that we have on every High Holiday. The richness of the mushrooms and avocado make this more than just an everyday salad. It's literally a meal in itself. It is meant to be served cold, but we prefer it hot. Either way, you will love it!

   3 tablespoons olive oil
   1 large onion, minced
   1 pound fresh mushrooms, sliced
   ½ teaspoon salt
   ¼ teaspoon ground black pepper
   5 tablespoons non-dairy sour cream
   2 tablespoons mayonnaise
   3 medium-sized avocados
   ⅓ cup fresh lemon juice

Put the oil in a wide skillet and sauté the onion on medium-high heat until golden brown.
Add the sliced mushrooms, the salt and pepper and sauté for 1 minute on high heat. Remove skillet from heat.
Add the sour cream and the mayonnaise, and mix.
Peel the avocado and cut into ½-inch cubes. Mix with the lemon juice and add to the mushroom mixture. Cool.
Transfer to a serving platter, cover and refrigerate for 2 hours.
Serve cold with toasted bread.

Artichoke with Mushrooms & Pine Nuts

Makes 6 servings

½ cup olive oil
6 artichoke hearts, fresh or frozen, cut in half
1 celery root, cut up into quarters and cut into slices of ¼ inch
    (the white part)
2 fresh sage leaves, minced
¼ cup dry white wine
½ teaspoon salt
¼ teaspoon fresh ground black pepper
2 garlic cloves, minced
1 big onion, minced
10 ounces fresh mushrooms cut up into quarters
⅓ cup pine nuts, sautéed in a little olive oil
2 tablespoons chopped parsley for garnish

Put half of the amount of oil in a frying pan.
Add the artichokes, the celery and the sage leaves.
Steam while stirring for about 5 minutes.
Add the wine and half the amount of the salt and pepper.
Bring to a boil and cook on a low heat for 10 minutes until the vegetables become sufficiently soft.
Put the rest of the oil in an additional frying pan and steam the garlic and the onion.
Increase the heat. Add the mushrooms. Sauté until brown. Add the remaining salt and pepper.
Put the mushrooms at the center of the serving platter. Arrange the artichoke and the celery around the mushrooms. Spread pine nuts on the top and garnish with parsley.
Serve hot.

Pineapple & Mushroom Salad

Makes 6 servings

1 cup pineapple from 14-ounce can of pineapple
1 7-ounce can of sliced mushrooms
1 8-ounce can baby corn, strained and sliced
½ small onion, cut into small cubes
4 tablespoons light mayonnaise
4 tablespoons pineapple juice from can
2 tablespoons confectioners' sugar
¼ teaspoon salt

Strain the pineapple, cut into cubes, and transfer to a serving bowl; add the mushrooms, the corn and the onion.
In separate bowl, mix the mayonnaise, the pineapple juice, the confectioners' sugar and the salt.
Pour on the salad, cover, and refrigerate to blend flavors for 2 hours. Serve cold.

Lentil & Spinach Stew

Makes 6 servings

1 ¼ cups green or brown lentils
4 tablespoons olive oil
1 large onion, minced
2 garlic cloves, minced
Salt and black pepper
1 teaspoon ground coriander seeds
1 pound fresh spinach, chopped
1 cup coriander leaves, minced
Juice from 1 lemon

Cover the lentils with water and cook until it becomes soft (you can soak them in water for about two hours before cooking). Strain.
In a saucepan, heat the oil and sauté the onion and the garlic until it is golden brown.
Add the salt, pepper and the coriander seeds and sauté while stirring another minute.
Add the spinach and the coriander leaves and cook on a very low heat. Cover the pan and cook for 10 minutes. Add the lemon juice and the cooked lentil, stir and cook another 5 minutes.
Serve hot or cold.

SUBSTITUTES

Salt Substitute

8 teaspoons sesame seeds
1 teaspoon salt
1 teaspoon rice

In small frying pan, toast the sesame lightly.
Place the toasted sesame in blender. Add the salt and blend well.
Transfer to an airtight jar.
To prevent moisture, add the rice to the mixture and shake well.
The combination of the sesame and the salt gives the flavor of sodium.
Use as any salt for cooking, salad, etc.

Mayonnaise Substitute

Makes 1 cup

1 8-ounce container plain yogurt
¼ teaspoon powdered mustard
1 teaspoon minced dill

Place all ingredients in a bowl.
Mix well.
Use as a low- calorie, sodium-free mayonnaise.